MAYBE TOMORROW

THOUGHTS, PRAYERS AND SMILES
FOR THE END OF EACH DAY

WITH

TONY MILES

FOREWORD BY
PAM RHODES

CWR

For Dad
– with thanks for your love,
generosity and practical help over the years.

Also with thanksgiving to God for the lives of
Mollie Elborough,
John Dyer,
John Robins,
and also those who died whilst sleeping rough
on the streets of London
– not known to me, but all known and loved by God.

THANK YOU for buying this book.
The author will be giving a proportion of his fee and of any
other profits he makes to support the work of The Passage.
You can read more about the work of this
Christian charity on page 188.

'A well-spent day brings happy sleep …'
Leonardo Da Vinci
– Italian Renaissance polymath (1452–1519)

COMMENDATIONS

'We are indeed all "work in progress"! *Maybe Tomorrow* is an accessible book; allowing one to dip in to a much needed oasis at the end of each busy day, to help nurture this work, to build some quality time into our day, and to prepare for the next.'
Mick Clarke, CEO The Passage

'What can I say about the voice of Tony Miles? It's his rich smile of a voice that brings Radio 2's *Pause for Thought* to life. It's his gentle, walk-with-me voice that draws alongside like a pilgrim. It's his coaxing, enquiry of a voice that asks the compelling questions. It's the sheer humanity of his voice that makes him such a rare and valued friend on the journey. Tony Miles has found his voice in *Maybe Tomorrow*. I hope you will find it as helpful as I do.'
Brian Draper, writer, thinker and speaker – including BBC Radio 4's
Thought for The Day

'I wish I had come up with *Maybe Tomorrow*! This is an accessible and refreshing book of reflections and insights which draws us to pray about heavy issues with a light touch.'
Joel Edwards, Director, Micah Challenge International

'Feeling miserable? Faith flagging a bit? Want to keep it that way? ON NO ACCOUNT read Tony's book!'
Andrew Graystone, Director of the Church and Media Network

'The wonderful Tony Miles has done it again ... I was looking forward to enjoying this book as a general read, but once more (as with *Maybe Today*) I found myself being gently ministered to in that generous, winsome way that is the hallmark of Tony Miles. Thanks Tony for another EXCELLENT and much needed book – I'll be taking this little gem with me everywhere!'
Diane Louise Jordan, TV & radio presenter

'Tony Miles is back with another compendium of insights and thoughts that will stimulate your day and get your brain moving in mysterious ways. He is a great communicator and the observations are fresh. If you want to be inspired – buy this book.'
Peter Kerridge, CEO Premier Christian Media

'We can so easily get swept along in life, so easily get drowned out. Yet *Maybe Tomorrow* stands still in the crowd and calls for silence in the chaos. Read it, absorb it, live it – because tomorrow might be too late.'
Michael O'Neill, CEO of Stewardship

'We are in many ways a "world gone mad". Like a cool drink on a hot day, *Maybe Tomorrow* calls you to a quiet centre in the midst of the maddening crowd and becomes a vehicle of God's inward grace. Honest, articulate, and faith-filled – Tony's book is a gift of God to God's people.'
Revd Mike Rayson, Pastor, Bethalto United Methodist Church, Bethalto Illinois USA

'Tony Miles has the great gift of taking the ordinary and opening up divine insight through it. This is an earthed book, no one will fail to be encouraged through it.'
Martin Turner, Team Leader and Superintendent Minister, Methodist Central Hall, Westminster.

CONTENTS

FOREWORD

Now I come to think of it, there are too many occasions in every day when I put things to one side to think about tomorrow. That's not through laziness – honest! Quite the opposite in fact, because it seems to me that I start each day at a gallop, and then race my way through every minute until my head hits the pillow at night. But then modern-day life is like that – not just for working mums like me, but for all of us. There's constant pressure at every level on our time and energy. Whether the main challenge for you comes from the dedication you must contribute simply to remain in work in an ever-decreasing job market – or whether it's the never-ending needs of home life that leave you exhausted at the end of the day – time flies, moments are lost and opportunities missed.

And the things we put off to tomorrow aren't just the practical chores that demand a physical action from us. We're also inclined to put off anything that challenges us on an emotional and spiritual level too. If something requires too much thought or pricks our conscience in an uncomfortable way, it's easier to push it to one side. Maybe tomorrow we'll give it the consideration it deserves. We're far too busy being busy to deal with it right now!

When we behave like that, Tony Miles describes us in this book as being less like a 'human being' and more like a 'human doing'! What a great way to put it – and what a talent Tony has for finding just the right phrase to make us sit up and think! He manages to put his finger on the heart of our concerns and conscience in a way that not only shows his skill as an author, but makes this book a real gem.

In some ways, *Maybe Tomorrow* feels delightfully domestic as day after day we learn more about Tony, his wife Frances and their two children in short tales of their everyday life which have a familiar ring to many of us. Through small experiences and observations, Tony pinpoints some of those emotional and spiritual challenges that the rest of us often choose to ignore, and then sums up in one line what we could do – maybe tomorrow – to face that challenge ourselves. Knowing how difficult that may be, he gives us some valuable tools to work with. He picks out just the right verse from the Bible to give us guidance and encouragement. He recognises that words can be elusive when we try to express our feelings in prayer, so he suggests a 'Night Prayer' which may well stay in our minds throughout the hours we sleep, and be our first thought in the new day. And then he finishes by drawing from his extensive knowledge of the writings, thoughts and musings of some of the great minds of the world to quote poems, readings and funny, touching stories which throw their own illuminating light on the challenges that face us.

This book is a toolkit for body, mind and soul, a companion for the journey. Keep it by your side and dip into it often – and then when you're busy, it's more likely to be on things that really count.

Pam Rhodes
Presenter, BBC Television's *Songs of Praise*

PREFACE

As you read this anthology of reflections, I hope I won't come across as an annoying super-spiritual kind of guy who's got his faith and devotional life 'all sorted' and in a healthy rhythm. The truth is, I'm very much 'work in progress'. My aim is to write honestly, recognising my own struggles when it comes to life, prayer and reflection. I merely share some insights gleaned along the way, hoping you'll find time to read my thoughts and will identify with some very random reflections. I have also included material gathered from many good friends and other sources – including a section of additional prayers and hymns towards the end of the book. My prayer is you will find God speaking to you through these pages, enabling you to pray as you prepare to sleep and make resolutions for the day ahead. What's more, I have tried to write accessibly and with a light touch, aspiring to avoid adding to a pile of excellent and worthy Christian books that are, sadly, rarely read.

THANKS

First and foremost, I am indebted to my wonderful wife, Frances. She is a constant companion, realistic encourager, and remarkable woman of faith. Without her this book wouldn't have been written. Not only did we arrive at the concept together (as you will read in the introduction), but Frances is also a loyal helper and constant source of inspiration too. Darling, we're a good team and I couldn't do all I do without you!

Once again I wish to record my appreciation of those who have run with the idea to put together another book when, if we're honest, we're probably all too busy. With grace and patience, friends and family have been a steady source of encouragement and practical help. THANK YOU ALL, including:

Family – my children, Hannah and Jonathan, for putting up with their dad – I'm very proud of you both. I mention Hannah especially for her excellent @daily_encourage Twitter thoughts: www.twitter.com/daily_encourage. (Do take a look at her blog: www.tellthemilovethem.com)

Dad, for his practical help; brother-in-law and prayer partner, John Izzard, for being a 'Barnabas'; and Best Man, Peter Bisley, for his friendship and support over many years.

Brian Draper, for his wisdom, care and inspiration.

Ministerial colleagues at Methodist Central Hall, Westminster, for their friendship, advice and good humour. I wish to single out our team leader and Superintendent Minister, the Revd Martin Turner, for enabling me to grow in my ministry and for his trust and friendship. Among many others I could mention at MCHW, I include the Revd Dr Malcolm White, the Revd Gordon Newton, Sister Denise Creed, and Revd Joanne Cox.

Proof-readers: Ali Burnett and Kaye Lee, for their attention to detail.

Friends at The Nationwide Christian Trust, especially Ray George and Canon Michael Cole, for allowing me to adapt a few thoughts that were originally written for past editions of *Living Light*.

Many other friends who have generously written prayers to be included, or words to commend the book. I am very grateful.

Pam Rhodes, for kindly writing the Foreword.

OMISSIONS

Except where original, or specifically acknowledged, other information included in this anthology is believed to be common knowledge or its origin is unknown. The sources of this material are many and varied. Some illustrations, quotes and jokes have been noted after hearing people use them in conversations, sermons and other contexts – including emails, the internet and Christian publications (such as local church magazines). I am grateful for this material and any omissions of acknowledgement will be gladly corrected publicly on my blog (www.tonymiles.com/blog) and in future editions of this book. Where there is need for clarification, material I have written has the initials *TM*.

Tony Miles

PRAYER:

O Lord, Alpha and Omega, who is there at life's beginnings and endings, may these reflections remind me of Your presence at the day's end. As I read, help me to find rest and peace in the security of Your loving embrace. Amen.

INTRODUCTION
WHAT A DAY!

'Life seems but a quick succession of busy nothings.'
Jane Austen – English novelist (1775–1817), from Mansfield Park

I start with confession ... 'it's good for the soul' ... apparently!

Once upon a time there was a BAD day. It began early with a dash to catch the 6.33am train and a fairly uneventful commute to St. James's Park Underground station. From there I walked to Methodist Central Hall, Westminster, taking in the fabulous view of Westminster Abbey en route. I climbed up the stairs to the third floor and entered my office out of breath at about 7.35am. A manic day then kicked off through until nearly 9pm. I hardly had time to pray, read or eat – only stopping to snatch a thirty-minute lunch break in Wesley's Café when my brother, Steve, popped in to visit. My thirteen-hour working day had been unrelenting: phone calls, emails, meetings, visitors and so on. At the end of it, I was exhausted and, apart from meeting up with my brother, I can't honestly say I'd done anything I had intended to do or taken any exercise. Mostly I'd been responding to the demands of others and a host of other unscheduled stuff. I felt terribly guilty I hadn't really spent enough time with God, my colleagues, or those I love.

'Rejoice with your family in the beautiful land of life!'
Albert Einstein – German-born American physicist (1879–1955)

Having said all this, I did meet my wife, Frances – albeit at 9pm! She'd had a hectic day too as a senior manager for a Christian charity. Despite worries and stresses of her own, she had dashed up to London for a church meeting. We had arranged to meet afterwards – neither of us having eaten properly. We decided to treat ourselves and went to Colosseo – a little Italian restaurant along Victoria Street. The waitress sat us down at a 'secluded and romantic table for two' ... right by the window. Nevertheless, we were able to watch the world going by as we sipped our drinks and waited for our food. We were both extremely tired and it was good to forget we still had the journey home ahead, and instead take time to offload our mutually frustrating days. Eventually a delicious and fairly extravagant meal arrived and we were just about to tuck in when we saw a disturbing sight just outside the window. There were a couple of unkempt homeless men rooting through a bin, trying to find food and rescue cardboard for their bedding. And we thought *we'd* had a bad day.

> 'And homeless near a thousand homes I stood,
> And near a thousand tables pined and wanted food.'
> William Wordsworth – English Romantic poet (1770–1850)

WHY 'MAYBE TOMORROW'?

'Today is the tomorrow you worried about yesterday.' Anon.

It was late when Frances and I eventually travelled home together on London's Underground. We turned our attention from our own preoccupations to the thin piece of glass that had separated two very different worlds. Yes, we'd both had a challenging day, but at least we had eaten and were returning to the warmth and security of our home and the company of family. We felt deeply for those who were going to be on the streets that night and resolved to do something to help the work of The Passage – a Christian organisation with a mission to help homeless people in Westminster. We pondered how could we have so much, yet sometimes let our lives become out of control and unsatisfying. What's more, had we become self-centred and numb to the need that was staring us in the face?

'You could write something about this,' suggested Frances. Her words got me thinking, and as I watched her flicking through her diary and pondering yet another busy day ahead, I had the idea of writing this book. Why? Well, firstly, I guess we are not the only Christians who sometimes get our life out of balance and need to reflect at the end of the day and make resolutions for the day ahead. And secondly, it might be a way of highlighting the plight of homelessness and raising a little bit of money in the process.

It would be good to try and make a difference. But what could I call such a book? Frances immediately suggested making it a sequel to my last book, *Maybe Today*. We laughed as we shared together some inappropriate book titles. Then my beloved came up with *Maybe Tomorrow*. Genius! Except, I didn't like the idea. I'm not one for putting off to tomorrow what could be done today. I thought 'Maybe Tomorrow' might give the impression that there could be a *mañana* element to faith: that there was an indefinite time for things to be done in the future, rather than grabbing the opportunity now. After all, there is a Spanish proverb, 'Tomorrow is the busiest day of the week'. I also recalled an autobiography by the broadcaster Ray Moore entitled *Tomorrow is Too Late*. Thankfully, Frances gave me another perspective and corrected me with a smile – she's usually right (but don't let her know):

1. What have we been doing? We've been reflecting on our day and making resolutions and prayers for the day ahead. Some things take time.

    'You cannot escape the responsibility of tomorrow by evading it today.' Abraham Lincoln –Sixteenth President of the United States (1809–1865)

2. Maybe we do need to rationalise our days and put off some things in order to be closer to God, more effective, and fulfilled too.

    'Learn from yesterday, live for today, hope for tomorrow. The important thing is not to stop questioning.' Albert Einstein – German-born American physicist (1879–1955)

And so, a bad day gave birth to this anthology. I could hardly sleep that night as I began forming the pages that follow in my head. In the silence of the night hours, I felt I was in God's presence and that He had my attention. In a strange and unexpected way, I knew God was telling me something. In response, I resolved to make some changes to my lifestyle in order to get my life more in balance and possibly a little more in tune with the rhythms our Creator has given us.

So, the very next day, I rang CWR and said, 'How about it?' If you are reading this, I must thank them for saying 'Yes.'

I hope readers of this book will be helped to close each day well and also take time to prepare for the next. When I'm weary and empty, I find it's good to remember God's mercy and help in the past, and to seek a deeper communion with Him in the future. This is what David was doing in the following psalm:

A PSALM OF DAVID, WRITTEN WHEN HE WAS IN THE DESERT OF JUDAH.

You, God, are my God, earnestly I seek you;
I thirst for you, my whole being longs for you,
in a dry and parched land where there is no water.
I have seen you in the sanctuary and beheld your power and
 your glory.
Because your love is better than life, my lips will glorify you.
I will praise you as long as I live, and in your name I will lift up
 my hands.
I will be fully satisfied as with the richest of foods; with singing
 lips my mouth will praise you.
On my bed I remember you; I think of you through the watches of
 the night.
Because you are my help, I sing in the shadow of your wings.
I cling to you; your right hand upholds me.
Psalm 63:1–8 (NIV, 2011)

A Prayer:
God of our days, nights, and tomorrows,
 Let Your Holy Spirit breathe upon the reflections in this book, that by Your grace and mercy,
 all who take time to ponder with honesty and openness may find rest, refreshment, and LIFE in all its fullness. In Jesus' name, I pray. Amen.

AT THE END OF AN OVERLY BUSY DAY

Jesus, I feel absolutely exhausted!
It's been one of those days: a long and relentless day;
a day when things haven't gone according to plan;
when I've not been in control;
when it seems time has been stolen and not reclaimed;
when I've loved in Your name
yet hardly had time for those I love the most.

As I look in the mirror my colour seems to have drained away,
Do I really look like that?
(even when I smile at the ageing balding one before me!)
My sparkle seems to have gone and my eyes are heavy.
To be honest, I'm hungry, tired and emotionally fragile.

Don't get me wrong, Lord,
my sighs are not out of hopelessness or despairing ... I trust YOU!
I just don't trust ME – that I've actually got my life in balance.
I fear I'm living on my own resources
and not tapping into the more You have for me.
I feel completely spent.
I can't say everything's been bad – just too much!
I can't say I've not been doing what You called me to do
... but all in one day, Lord?

Jesus, did You ever feel like that?
Did You ever get compassion fatigue?
Did people ever wind You up,
so You had to count to 100 rather than 10,
or to draw rather more circles in the sand than You intended?
I guess You did.
Did You ever go to sleep wondering if You'd manage another day,
or perhaps go back to carpentry?
I guess You did. I hope You did.
But, Son of Man, I'm glad You didn't!

Do you know what keeps me hopeful, Lord?
It's that our Father gave us the gift of rest;
it's that Your Holy Spirit can re-create people like me;
it's that You were always obedient;
and are in the resurrection business!

So, as I let this manic day slip away,
I hand whatever I have done, or not done, to You.
I ask You to repair me:
mentally, emotionally, physically and spiritually.
As I sleep, minister to my soul gently
and renew my calling – my inner passion to serve You …
and Yours.

I'm running out of coherent sentences, Lord,
so accept my rambling,
I think I've used up all today's allowance of meaningful words!
I want to listen to You instead,
but to be frank, I've heard enough for one day
… unless You keep it short, Lord.
 'I love You!' is enough for me tonight.

Jesus, may tomorrow be better, for You … and for me.
May I learn from my mistakes
and look after myself, as well as caring for others,
for I can't help them if I'm done in!

Remind me, Lord,
that your Word did NOT say,
'I have come that you may be done in',
but that Your coming had to do with LIFE.

Maybe tomorrow, I will find the MORE in fuller measure.
As for now … PEACE be with my loved ones.
(I should have treated them better today!)
Thank You that they love me for who I am,

and can look beyond what I do and all my shortcomings.
I wonder where they get that from, Lord?

Maybe tomorrow, I can rediscover the 'unforced rhythms of grace',
and 'rise renewed in perfect love',
bright-eyed and bushy-tailed!
Not due to a superficial make-over,
or a short-lived energy boost,
but because Your inexhaustible resources
have been released into me once again,
with invigorating and life-giving power!

Now, thank You, Lord,
for I am eagerly anticipating the precious gift
of healing sleep … Amen … ZZzzz
TM

'Yesterday is but today's memory, and tomorrow is today's dream.'
Khalil Gibran – Lebanese–American artist, poet and writer (1883–1931)

EVENING QUIET TIME

It has been an ancient Christian practice to pray in the morning and in the evening – usually including the prayer Jesus taught us: 'The Lord's Prayer'. In the evenings there has also been a tradition of praying at sunset when lighting the lamps. This was to remember that Jesus Christ is the 'joyful light of God the Father'. Whether or not you are someone who is familiar with Vespers, Compline or having an evening 'Quiet Time', I offer this suggestion for how you could use this book devotionally. It's a simple structure for evening prayer that could be used regularly, occasionally, adapted, or even ignored if you prefer freestyle! If you are tired – please don't try to be too ambitious. I firmly believe heartfelt short prayers are better than not praying at all. Above all, don't feel guilty when you can't maintain your pattern of prayer. Remember, our heavenly Father is just delighted when you do spend time in His presence; the more you do, the more your relationship will grow.

SETTLE DOWN

For a few moments say one of the following phrases each time you breathe in deeply:

Come, Holy Spirit.
Jesus, my Saviour, have mercy on me.
Abba Father.
Maranatha! (Come, O Lord)

PRAYER

God of the day, the evening, and the night,
I draw close to You as I reflect on another day in the life You've given me.
Thank you for bringing me to the day's end;
thank you for Your grace and mercy – whether I have fully

appreciated it, or not.
Forgive my failures and shortcomings, in Jesus' name,
and help me now to turn towards Your love and light.
Speak to me by Your Holy Spirit as I read and pray,
that I may learn from my experiences
and be prepared to live for You tomorrow;
for the sake of Your kingdom. Amen.

TM

MAYBE TOMORROW

*Read one of the 50 reflections in the book with accompanying
Bible passages and other material.*

PRAYERS FOR YOURSELF AND OTHERS:

*Take time to think about what you have read and say your own
prayers focusing on some or all of the following areas:
World and national affairs
Your community
Your family
Yourself*

THE PRAYER OF THE KINGDOM:
THE LORD'S PRAYER

Our Father in heaven,
hallowed be Your name,
Your kingdom come,
Your will be done,
on earth as in heaven.
Give us today our daily bread.
Forgive us our sins
as we forgive those who sin against us.
Save us from the time of trial
and deliver us from evil.
For the kingdom, the power
and the glory are Yours,
now and for ever. Amen.

OPTIONAL

Choose an additional prayer, reading or hymn from pages 191–208.

CONCLUDING PRAYER

Choose one of the following:

O Lord, Light of the World, as I prepare to sleep and the night falls, help me to remember that 'the light shines in the darkness, and the darkness has not overcome it'. Amen.

Based on John 1:5, RSV

Lighten our darkness, Lord, *I* pray:
And in Your mercy defend *me* from all perils and dangers of this night;
For the love of Your only Son, *my* Saviour Jesus Christ. Amen.

*Gelasian Sacramentary, book of Christian liturgy, eighth century
(adapted for personal use)*

Lord, as I go to bed this night,
I thank You for my blessed life.
Thank You for my family,
Thank You for creating me.
For the world and all my friends,
And for Your love that never ends.
Protect me through the darkness of night,
Keep me in Your blessed sight.
Show me to another day,
Direct me to Your loving way.
Bring me into Jesus' arms,
So He may protect me from sin and harm.
Thank You and goodnight to You,
And Lord, may my love stay forever true. Amen.

Author unknown

RHYTHM AND REST

Tomorrow is the most important thing in life.
Comes to us at midnight very clean.
It's perfect when it arrives and it puts itself in our hands.
It hopes we've learnt something from yesterday.

John Wayne – stage name for Marion Mitchell Morrison. American film actor, director and producer (1907–1979)

01 EVERYDAY THIN PLACES

If you've flicked straight here without reading pages 11–12,
I don't blame you – it's the sort of thing I'd do! If you'd read
them, which I hope you'll do, there was among them the
tale of a manic, exhausting day. It ended with Frances and
I snatching an Italian meal and our being disturbed by the
sight of homeless people just inches away from us. They were
rummaging through a bin for food the other side of our
restaurant window:

> 'We turned our attention from our own preoccupations to the
> thin piece of glass that had separated two very different worlds.'

Sylvia Maddox is a retreat leader and she was the one who drew
my attention to a beautiful Celtic saying: '… heaven and earth are
only three feet apart, but in the thin places that distance is even
smaller. A thin place is where the veil that separates heaven and
earth is lifted and one is able to receive a glimpse of the glory of
God.'[1] Celtic Christians believed they lived on the borders of the
physical and the spiritual. In certain places it was as though they
could 'touch heaven' and experience something of God's glory
breaking through to challenge or inspire them. I wonder if this is
the sort of thing that happened on the Mount of Transfiguration,
when the Lord's clothes became blinding white.[2] I've certainly
encountered God more easily in places where people have
worshipped for generations. It's why people go on pilgrimage to
places like the Hebridean Isle of Iona, Lindisfarne Abbey on Holy
Island, or retreat houses, shrines and cathedrals, like Durham
and Winchester; and don't forget world pilgrimage sites, like St
Peter's Basilica (Rome, Italy), the Holy Land, or the Way of St
James (the Camino Santiago de Compostela, Spain). These are all
examples of what I call *special thin places*. But when Frances and

I were moved by seeing men scavenging for food as we ate our fill, the restaurant window became for us an 'everyday thin place' or a 'thin moment' – a deeply spiritual experience in an ordinary day.

MAYBE TOMORROW you could look out for 'everyday thin places' in your day. But watch out – it could be dangerous. God may use them to ruffle your feathers by challenging or inspiring you. The more you open your eyes and ears, the more 'thin places' you'll find – even in the familiar or the mundane.

NIGHT PRAYER:

Lord, I bring to you the poverty of my soul to be transformed by Your beauty; the wildness of my passions to be tamed by Your love; the stubbornness of my will to be conformed to Your commandments and the yearnings of my heart to be renewed by Your grace; both now and for ever. Amen.

St Catherine of Genoa – Italian Roman Catholic mystic, respected for her work among the sick and the poor (1447–1510)

BIBLE READING:

'You will seek me and find me when you seek me with all your heart.' **Jeremiah 29:13**
'One thing I ask of the LORD, this is what I seek: that I may dwell in the house of the LORD all the days of my life, to gaze upon the beauty of the LORD, and to seek him in his temple.' **Psalm 27**

FURTHER REFLECTION
BEING POLITICAL:

God of Justice, you hear the cries of the widow, the orphan and
the stranger;
Unblock my ears and eyes to the injustices of our world.

Christ who came to live among us, you feasted with prostitutes
and tax collectors;
Help me to love this confused and confusing world.

Holy Spirit, holy changemaker, you transform all that we are
and all we can be;
Encourage me to seek signs of your transformation in the most
hopeless situations of the world.

Help me to act for justice,
Love your people,
And be ready and willing to be part of your kingdom,
In the name of your Son, Amen.

Used with permission. Copyright © Rachel Lampard November 2011

@daily_encourage

God will meet us in His timing and as He chooses, but He's
never late!

Hannah Sarah Miles, twitter.com/@daily_encourage

SMILE:

POLITICS is the art of foretelling what will happen tomorrow,
next year, and being able to explain why it didn't happen.

Anon.

WHO AM I?

'I'd been responding to the demands of others and a host of other unscheduled stuff.'

On holiday once, I was asked, 'What do you do?' I didn't want to reply immediately. Saying 'I'm a Methodist minister' can sometimes be a real conversation-stopper. My family asked our new friends to hazard a guess. It was amusing seeing them try and work me out: policeman? Nightclub bouncer? Tax inspector? Used car salesman? They couldn't believe it when they heard the truth. It's funny how we judge people we don't know by how they look, and maybe with our own prejudices. There's a danger in finding one's value, or defining others by what we *do* alone. After all, what does it say about the unemployed?

There are times when my life feels out of control and I am a 'human doing', rather than a 'human being'! If I'm honest, I'm not always sure who's in control. Who dictates life's pace, busyness, and responsibilities? Too much of the craziness in my diary happens when I fail to be still before God and don't take a good honest look at my life. I'm learning to ask the question 'Who am I?' before I plan my days. The more I do this, the more I learn about myself and who it is that God is calling me to be in Christ.

Steve Jobs was an influential American entrepreneur and the co-founder of Apple. He sadly died after a long battle with cancer in 2011 at the age of 56. Just six years before he'd given a challenging speech to the graduates of Stanford University. Reflecting on his life he told them, 'Your time is limited, so don't waste it living someone else's life. Don't be trapped by dogma – which is living with the results of other people's thinking. Don't let the noise of others' opinions drown out your own inner voice. And most important, have the courage to follow your heart and intuition. They somehow already know what you truly want to become. Everything else is secondary.'[3]

MAYBE TOMORROW you could take a good look in the mirror when you wake up. Ask yourself some of these crucial questions: Who am I? Am I being true to myself and how I spend my time? Am I listening for the whisper of God's Holy Spirit within? Am I committed to regaining control of my life with God's help and by letting Him have control? Oh, and a tip … don't answer these questions too quickly!

NIGHT PRAYER:

Thank You for today, Lord, and for lessons learned. Help me to ask questions of myself tomorrow. Amen.

BIBLE READING:

'Trust in the LORD with all your heart and lean not on your own understanding; In all your ways acknowledge him, and he will make your paths straight.' **Proverbs 3:5–6**
The Vine and the Branches **John 15:1–17**

FURTHER REFLECTION
BEING PATIENT WHEN UNEMPLOYED:

This is a relentless journey of twists and turns that started a long time ago but seems to have no end. Following signposts where the route looked promising, leading to a destination full of adventure, interest and challenge but instead went nowhere. But I continue, plodding onwards, hopefully going somewhere.

I can choose to rise above this cloud of oppression, doubt and despair if I reach out and lean on the One who sees the bigger picture and who will weave all this disappointment and perplexity into His divine plan.

I will resolve to be focused and realistic about what I can do with the time I have and to use it wisely and well; learning to live life simply and to the full.

The future may be uncertain, but I need to keep persisting and trusting in a faithful God who knows and understands – even if I don't.

Used with permission. Copyright © Marian Izzard September 2011

@daily_encourage

'Guard your heart above all else, for it determines the course of your life.' (Prov. 4:23, NLT).

Hannah Sarah Miles

SMILE:

It's déjà vu all over again!

Lawrence Peter 'Yogi' Berra – former American baseball player and manager (1925–)

03 THE RHYTHM OF LIFE

'... I resolved to make some changes to my lifestyle in order to get my life more in balance and possibly a little more in tune with the rhythms our Creator has given us.'

I pulled up at the traffic lights and was waiting for a green signal. As I leaned on the steering wheel, I was playing 'air drums' and nodding in time to a great piece of pop music. After a while I glanced to my right and noticed a car had pulled into the lane next to me. The woman driver was obviously tuned into the same radio station. At first we were both embarrassed when we noticed each other getting carried away with the beat like a couple of Muppets! We smiled, realising we'd both got into the same song and were in fact in tune with each other.

I believe God created a world with rhythm at its heart: the pattern of the seasons, the movement of dawn to dusk each day, the ebb and flow of tides, the sequences in our bodies, including breathing and heartbeats, and the music in all cultures throughout the world. I could go on listing rhythmic patterns that I believe God has put into life. Just as George Gershwin composed a song 'I got rhythm', God's 'got' it too and it's in His creation – in you and in me. The trouble is, if we resist those natural pulses and prefer an unhealthy freestyle, we become offbeat; life can become discordant, disruptive, and even destructive. The secret is to discover, understand, and appreciate our Creator's rhythm. It not only helps us to be in harmony with Him and each other, but also to be caught up in the sacred dance He intended for us.

MAYBE TOMORROW you could consider the words of
the Trappist monk Thomas Merton (1915–1968): 'Happiness
is not a matter of intensity but of balance, order, rhythm and
harmony.' In fact, if your relationship comes in tune with God,
C.S. Lewis would argue that you will find something even more
lasting than happiness – you will find Joy flowing into every
part of your life.[4]

NIGHT PRAYER:

Lord of the Dance, forgive the times when my life has been all
over the place, more like a 'Dad at a disco' than the graceful
and joyful mover You'd have me be. Help me to listen to the
beat of my heart as I try to sleep. May I awake rested and ready
to listen for the beat of Your heart in the world. You lead and I
will follow. Amen.

BIBLE READING:

Jesus said 'Are you tired? Worn out? Burned out on religion?
Come to me. Get away with me and you'll recover your life. I'll
show you how to take a real rest. Walk with me and work with
me – watch how I do it. Learn the unforced rhythms of grace.
I won't lay anything heavy or ill-fitting on you. Keep company
with me and you'll learn to live freely and lightly.'
Matthew 11:28–30, *The Message*
The Beginning **Genesis 1:1–31**

FURTHER REFLECTION
BEING CAUGHT UP IN THE LIFE OF GOD:

In his book *Mere Christianity*, C. S. Lewis wrote: '… In
Christianity God is not a static thing – not even a person –
but a dynamic, pulsating activity, a life, almost a kind of drama.
Almost, if you will not think me irreverent, a kind of dance. The
union between the Father and Son is such a live concrete thing

that this union itself is a Person … What grows out of the joint life of the Father and Son is a real Person, is, in fact, the Third of the three Persons who are God … The whole dance, or drama, a pattern of this three-Personal life is to be played out in each one of us or (putting it the other way round) each one of us has got to enter that pattern, take his place in that dance.' [5]

Used with permission. C.S. Lewis, Mere Christianity

'Music and rhythm find their way into the secret places of the soul.'
Plato – Classical Greek philosopher and mathematician (400 BC)

@daily_encourage
'If I keep my eyes on GOD, I won't trip over my own feet.'
(Psa. 25:15, *The Message*).
Hannah Sarah Miles

SMILE:
There was a dance teacher who talked of a very old dance called 'The Politician'. 'All you have to do,' she told her class, 'is take three steps forward, two steps backward, then side-step, side-step, and turn around.'

Anon.

04

'I hardly had time to pray, read, or eat – only stopping to snatch a thirty-minute lunch break in Wesley's Café ...'

'So you think it's OK to break the Ten Commandments, Tony?' said Janet rather loudly as we chatted in the corridor. 'What, me? Never – honest!' Janet persisted, 'What day did you take off this week?' I waffled unsuccessfully and realised I had no excuse. It's an occupational hazard, but Sundays are rarely Sabbath days for ministers. My 'Lord's Day' is flexible – either a Tuesday or Saturday. I confess that on this occasion I hadn't taken either. I was grateful for the brutal honesty of a concerned friend. It's interesting I can sometimes feel guiltier about taking time for R&R than I do about breaking the fourth commandment. There's something wrong with me and with today's culture that thinks work, activity and achievement are better than time for re-creation. If God needed rest after six days, then I certainly do!

MAYBE TOMORROW, or on Sunday (or both), you can take time to smell the roses, chill out, and worship God.

NIGHT PRAYER:

Remind me, Lord, that I'm not made for the Sabbath; it was made for me. BUT, You did make me to rest. Amen.

BIBLE READING:

'Remember the Sabbath day by keeping it holy. Six days you shall labour and do all your work, but the seventh day is a Sabbath to the LORD your God. On it you shall not do any work ...' **Exodus 20:8–10**
A Sabbath-Rest for the People of God **Hebrews 4:1–11**

FURTHER REFLECTION
BEING IN BALANCE:

The Lord is my Pace-Setter
I shall not rush.
He makes me stop and rest for quiet intervals.
He provides for me with images of stillness
which restore my serenity.
He leads me in ways of efficiency
Through calmness of mind,
And His guidance is Peace.
Even though I have a great many things
to accomplish each day
I will not fret
For His presence is here.
His timelessness,
His all-importance,
Will keep me in balance.
He prepares refreshment and renewal
in the midst of my activity
by anointing my head
with His oils of tranquillity.
My cup of joyous energy overflows.
Surely harmony and effectiveness
Shall be the fruits of my hours
For I shall walk
In the place of my Lord
And dwell in His house
For ever.

A Japanese version of the Twenty-third Psalm by Toki Miyashina

@daily_encourage

Why don't you take a moment to look around God's creation today? It might help put things into perspective. ☺

Hannah Sarah Miles

SMILE:

Do not feel totally, personally, irrevocably responsible for everything. That's my job! Love, God!

Anon.

05 TOO TIRED TO SLEEP?

'We were both extremely tired and it was good to forget we still had the journey home ahead ...'

When my children were babies, I remember occasions when Frances and I were desperately trying to get them to sleep, but they were over-tired. Instead of peacefully nodding off as we read them a story or played the 'Sleep sound in Jesus' music, they would have none of it – exercising their lungs instead. Frustrating, when *we* were so tired.

Most of the time I don't have a problem sleeping, though there are occasions when I lie awake wishing I could sleep, but can't. I think Frances experiences this more than me – and it's not just my snoring that's the issue.

Minds and hearts can be full of stuff: work or family worries, health concerns or pain, guilt or regrets, anger or grief, loneliness or depression, and so on. The more such thoughts and emotions go round and round in your head, the more awake you become. Then you worry about not sleeping – and that makes matters worse.

People try all sorts of things: a late hot milky drink; a brisk walk or some other exercise to wear them out; and others, rightly or wrongly, turn to pills. For the Christian, there's something else to try. I commend what you may be doing right now, and that's having an evening 'quiet time': for reading, meditation or prayer. That's not praying about getting to sleep, but helping to prepare for sleep; not so much fighting the problem, but engaging in 'diversionary tactics' and leaning on God's breast, as it were – the ultimate Giver of sleep and peace.

When at theological college, I occasionally attended a service of 'Compline' (or 'Complan', as I affectionately called it!). It was a blend of nutritious readings and prayers at the end of the day – a mixture of psalms of protection against spiritual powers and prayers of love and trust to ease people into sleep. When I was stressing over incomplete essays and pressing deadlines, I found it a helpful way of getting things in perspective and finding elusive peace and rest.

MAYBE TOMORROW you'll be better able to face the day if you follow John MacArthur's advice: when asked if he counted sheep when he couldn't sleep, he answered, 'No. I talk to the Shepherd.'

NIGHT PRAYER:

Father God, help me to come to You in prayer, as Christians have done for generations, and find refreshing rest. Let me discover a devotional rhythm that can help rock me in the cradle of Your love and peace. Amen.

BIBLE READING:

Jesus said, 'Come to me, all you who are weary and burdened, and I will give you rest.' **Matthew 11:28**
Lie down and sleep in peace **Psalm 4:8**

FURTHER REFLECTION
BEING DISCIPLINED WHEN IT COMES
TO SLEEP:

'If physical energy is the foundation of all dimensions of
energy, sleep is the foundation of physical energy. No single
behaviour more fundamentally influences our effectiveness in
waking life. Sleep deprivation takes a toll on our health, our
emotional well-being, and our cognitive functioning.'[6]

*Tony Schwartz – President and CEO of the Energy Project,
www.theenergyproject.com*

Try to develop a pattern of at least seven to nine hours of
sleep, where possible. Remember that regular exercise helps
sleep, but other things we think might help, like alcohol, don't
give us the sort of sleep we need. Tony Schwartz talks about
'parking anxieties' as being a 'powerful way to calm your mind
and get a better night's sleep.'[7]

@daily_encourage

Amazing things begin to happen when you put your whole life
in God's hands. In fact, it's the safest place you could be.

Hannah Sarah Miles

SMILE:

What question can never be answered with 'yes'?
Are you asleep?

Anon.

EAT SMART

'We had arranged to meet afterwards – neither of us having eaten properly.'

Many years ago, Frances and I were part of a beach mission team in Marazion, Cornwall. It's a lovely part of the world and the locals extended warm and generous hospitality. The trouble was, each time a different family fed us they said, 'You must have a proper Cornish pasty – not like those shop-bought ones.' They were fantastic, but you can have too much of a good thing. We subtly asked the food co-ordinator if we could possibly cut down on the pasties. The next day was Sunday and we were served a delicious roast for lunch. Five hours later, after a busy afternoon in the sun, we went to another host. She was terribly apologetic. 'I'm sorry, my lovelies,' she said, 'I hear you've had too many pasties – so I've got a treat for you. I've made you a big roast dinner!' Politely, we ate very well – I was reminded of a certain Christmas episode of *The Vicar of Dibley*.

Overindulging too often isn't good for one's health. The rising number of people who are obese in Britain is worrying. After Christmas a few years ago, I decided to do something about my weight and actually managed to lose a couple of stone. It wasn't easy, but I felt so much better for it. One thing I learnt was that eating well didn't just involve cutting down on food. When busy I used to eat badly and irregularly. I would often skip breakfast because I didn't feel like eating early in the morning. Then I'd get to work and before long it would be lunchtime and I wouldn't have eaten – apart from snacking on biscuits to keep me going. Yes, I'd then eat a good lunch, but would work through into the evening, arriving home having not eaten at teatime. This meant I was eating very late again. And so the cycle went on. The 'new me' tries to eat breakfast, lunch and tea, and nothing heavy late at night. It does work! It cuts down

the desire to snack on rubbish between meals. I love my food
and I'm no saintly eater, but I've learnt the hard way that smart
and disciplined eating works – just like my mum said it would.

MAYBE TOMORROW you could decide whether you need
to improve your diet or eating patterns.

NIGHT PRAYER:

God my Provider, I thank You that I've had food to eat today.
Help me to eat responsibly and not to take what I have for
granted. May I be mindful of those who are hungry and thirsty,
and give generously to help them. Amen.

BIBLE READING:

'So whether you eat or drink or whatever you do, do it all for
the glory of God.' **1 Corinthians 10:31**
'Out of the most severe trial, their overflowing joy and their
extreme poverty welled up in rich generosity. For I testify that
they gave as much as they were able, and even beyond their
ability ... See that you also excel in this grace of giving ...'
2 Corinthians 8:1–15

FURTHER REFLECTION
BEING PRAYERFUL FOR AN ALIEN CONTINENT:

Lord,
I pray for those
for whom tomorrow is an alien continent
flowing with clean water and enough to eat;
Where mothers live to hold their babies and children live long
enough to go to school.
Where diseases die out, the weak are protected without a bribe,
 And the soil smiles with the sky.

And Lord,
I pray that I might act:
To speak for those who can only dream – and wish they would
not wake.
Let me give or go.
Let me shout or shake my fists.
Fill me with angry hope
to see their dream come true.

Used with permission. Copyright © Revd Dr Joel Edwards
5 November 2011 (Jos Nigeria) www.micahchallenge.org

@daily_encourage

The world will make you feel stupid and inadequate. Yet only
God's opinion matters.

Hannah Sarah Miles

SMILE:

The Garlic Diet: You don't lose weight, you just look thinner
from a distance.

Anon.

07 FIT?

'... I can't honestly say I'd done anything I had intended to do or any exercise.'

At Methodist Central Hall, Westminster, we offer blood pressure checks once a month after worship. It's a free service offered by qualified practice nurses in our congregation. They don't give out advice or diagnosis, but if there are problems they will suggest that people book an appointment with their GP. It's amazing how often irregularities have been discovered. To set a good example, I confidently went to have my heart rate checked. I ended up seeing my doctor. It wasn't a serious problem, but I clearly needed to make changes to my lifestyle. My daily work is very sedentary – apart from exercising the tongue! I now try to work up a sweat at least three times a week – either at the gym or swimming. There are times when I don't keep to my routine, and I always suffer for it. When I'm physically fitter, I'm less prone to illness, better able to cope with stress, and more creative and productive. A European health review revealed that almost a quarter of British women are obese and nearly as many men. Yet exercise scientists examining research have revealed it's better, in terms of the risk of mortality, to be overweight and active, than normal weight and inactive.[8] Another twelve-year study disclosed that older adults who exercised just once a week were 40% less likely to die during the study period than those who did nothing. Just 30 minutes of exercise a day can make a huge difference to the body God has entrusted to you!

Now that swimming is part of my health rhythm, my good friend Brian Draper encouraged me to use the time to 'practise the presence of God'. He said, 'Try not to think about anything. If thoughts arise, let them go but don't follow them. Ask yourself instead, what does the water feel like? How does my body feel? What do I notice about my movement through the water? What sounds can I hear? How can I enjoy being present to this one length, instead of wishing I was at the end? Otherwise, simply focus on your breathing.'[9] I love doing this. I then imagine looking down on my life and consider what God thinks about me in His love, concern and compassion. It helps me get things into perspective.

MAYBE TOMORROW you can get your heart pumping for Jesus – in more ways than one! It just might enable you to be better equipped to make the most of the precious gift of life you've been given.

NIGHT PRAYER:

Life-giving God, thank You for the heart and body You have given me. Help me to keep fit, that I may be able serve You and others more effectively. Amen.

BIBLE READING:

'Do you not know that your body is a temple of the Holy Spirit, who is in you, whom you have received from God? You are not your own; you were bought at a price. Therefore honour God with your body.' **1 Corinthians 6:19-20**
You are God's holy temple **1 Corinthians 3:9,16–17**

FURTHER REFLECTION
BEING IN GOOD SHAPE ALL ROUND:

'All the systems in our body pulse rhythmically when we're healthy – heart rate, brain waves, body temperature, blood pressure, hormone levels. "It would be reasonable to say," explains the chronobiologist Josephine Arendt, "that everything that happens in our bodies is rhythmic until proven otherwise."

Our most fundamental need is to spend and renew energy.
We breathe in, and we breathe out. We can't do one for very
long without doing the other, and the more deeply we do both,
the better we operate, not just physically but also mentally
and emotionally.'[10]

Tony Schwartz – President and CEO of the Energy Project, www.theenergyproject.com

@daily_encourage

An intimate friendship with God will not only strengthen you,
but will guide and carry you through rough times.

Hannah Sarah Miles

SMILE:

I don't exercise at all. If God had wanted me to touch my toes
He would have put them up higher on my body.

Anon.

BEING A 'GOD-GAZER'

I would like to thank Malcolm Duncan for allowing me to publish God-Gazer *which had a significant impact on me – I have prayed it fervently many times!* TM

I want to be a *God-gazer,*
captured by the brilliance
that springs from the radiance
of You.

I want to be a God-gazer!
Not a cheap food grazer
or an easy option lazer.
I want to be a trail-blazer
for the ordinary, everyday life.

I want to be a God-gazer –
not just copying the halcyon ways
that shimmer brighter in the haze
of by-gone rays and the good old days.

I want to be a God-gazer!
Looking beyond the trappings of success,
cutting through the stucco of respectability
like a laser piercing darkness.

I want to be a God-gazer!
Reaching for the stars and
seeing beauty in the moment by
becoming fluent in the language
of the God Who is here, Who is now.

I want to be a God-gazer
until my imagination is saturated;
until my thirst is sated;
until my passion is stirred;
until my intellect is stretched
as far as it can be;
until my yearning yearns
for others to be free.

I want to be a God-gazer –
not a meetings manager
or a people pleaser
or a 'tea and sympathy' vicar –
not a leadership trainer,
not just a speaker
but a seeker.

I want to be a God-gazer ...
and for a moment I want God
to gaze through me.
I want others to see
His eyes
Heart
Mind
and Love
above everything else in me.

I want to be a God-gazer
captured by the brilliance
that springs from the radiance
of You.

Life-giver!
I want to be a Life-giver
not a life-sucker.
I want my life to be releasing
not appeasing or placating.

I want to be a Life-giver,
A drainpipe without blockages,
A circuit without stoppages,
A connector without breakages.

I want to be a Life-giver!
A 'you can do it' releaser,
A 'have a go' preacher,
A 'you were born to do this' pastor.

I want to be a Life-giver –
Seeing rivers flow, not die,
Seeing others rise and fly,
Helping friends reach for the stars
even if they sometimes miss.
At least they can say they tried.

I want to be a Life-giver,
Generous in spirit and in heart,
Letting the forgotten make a start
at being Life-givers, too.

I want to be a Life-giver
because I am a God-gazer
not because it's about me
but because it's about Him
because life can't spring
from any other 'thing'.

I want to be a Life-giver
connected to the Source
and pointing to the Son –
standing in the shadow of the Light
celebrating Him.

World-changer.
I want to be a World-changer
not just a furniture re-arranger
or an 'it could be better' winger
or a 'have the leftovers' stinger.

I want to be a World-changer!
A doer, not just a talker.
I want to spread the clothes of heaven,
No more or less than a poor man's dreams,
beneath the feet of Jesus.

I want to be a World-changer –
'Cos on a morning many winters ago
the tomb was open
and the curse was broken.
Death had to let go
and re-creation burst out
of an old wineskin
like water from a geyser,
Like the cry of a child
pushed into the world
and nothing
would shut Him up.

I want to be a World-changer
because it's started ...
because the vanguard's on the move ...
and love is pushing out hate
and light is shining out
and darkness can't understand it
beat it
change it
hide it
kill it
stop it
win.

I want to be a World-changer
because there's safety in this danger.
There's meaning in this purpose.
There's joy in this mission
and too many others are missing
the power of life in all its fullness.

World-changer? Life-giver? God-gazer.
God, break in – then break out
Fill – then make me leak.
Plug me in and push me out.
In me, through me, around me.
Make me a Patrick.
Make me a Brendan.
God-gazing, life-giving, world-changing.
Captured by the brilliance
that springs from the radiance
of You.

PEACE AND JOY

'Do not be afraid of tomorrow; for God is already there.'
Anon.

SILENCE IS GOLDEN

08

'In the silence of the night hours, I felt I was in God's presence and that He had my attention.'

Silence is increasingly rare these days. If things go silent, we presume something is wrong. Most radio stations have special software that will automatically play music from its playlist if there's a break in transmission. Unfortunately, in the early days of a radio station I know well, that's exactly what happened during a special broadcast: during the two minutes' silence one Remembrance Day the computer kicked in and played … 'O Happy Day'. Ouch. I doubt the phone lines were silent afterwards either!

I'm learning not to fear planned and unplanned silence. James, in his letter, writes, 'Submit yourselves, then, to God. Resist the devil, and he will flee from you. Come near to God and he will come near to you …' (James 4:7–8a). It's good to pause and let the silence speak; to let God speak; and to listen – beyond the noise.

MAYBE TOMORROW you could consider the Estonian proverb that says, 'Silence is sometimes the answer'.

NIGHT PRAYER:

When the world tells us we are what we do with our activity, acumen, or achievement,
let us learn we are what we do with our silence.
When the world tells us we are what we do with our spending power, selling power, or our power of speech,
let us learn we are what we do with our silence.

When the world tells us to drown the silent sufferings of others
with indifference or noise, or to forget the art of stillness even
in the storm,
let us learn we are what we do with our silence.
When the world tells us to rush in where angels fear to tread,
let us learn that angels listen first before they take a step
for the voice of God in the silence ...

Used with permission. Ruth Burgess, The Pattern of Our Days, *Copyright © Wild Goose Publications, The Iona Community, Glasgow, Scotland: 1996.*

BIBLE READING:

'For God alone my soul waits in silence; from him comes my
salvation.' **Psalm 62:1, NRSV**
Deep calls to deep **Psalm 42**

FURTHER REFLECTION
BEING STILL:

In silence
I listen for you,
in dark
I look for you,
with gloved hands
I feel for you,
in drought
I thirst for you.

When I unblock my ears,
open my eyes,
take off my gloves,
I hear you call,
see you standing, one hand
stretched out to hold mine,
the other offering
a chalice of clear cool water.

Used with permission. Copyright © Kaye Lee January 2012

@daily_encourage

Sometimes I forget I have a relationship with the Creator of the universe! What's remarkable is He WANTS a relationship with ME and YOU too!

Hannah Sarah Miles

SMILE:

Silence is not only golden; it is seldom misquoted.

Bob Monkhouse, English comedian, scriptwriter, games show host and actor (1928–2003)

09 SORRY TO BOTHER YOU

'In a strange and unexpected way, I knew God was telling me something.'

Has God ever spoken to you audibly? Well, He hasn't spoken to me that way – unless I wasn't listening at the time! However, when I am receptive, God does communicate with me in a whole variety of ways. Over the years, I've learnt to discern Him speaking to me through my reading, prayers, times of stillness, through creation, other people, and those little 'God-incidences', as I call them. I was feeling very low one difficult day, when one of my radio listeners sent me an email. It said they were just forwarding a letter to me:

Dear Friend,

How are you? I just had to send a note to tell you how much I love you and care about you. I saw you yesterday as you were talking with your friends. I waited all day hoping you would want to talk with me also. As evening drew near, I gave you a sunset to close your day and a cool breeze to rest you … and I waited. You never came. Oh yes, it hurts me … But I love you because I am your friend. I saw you fall asleep last night and longed to touch your brow, so I spilled moonlight upon your pillow and face. Again I waited, wanting to rush down so we could talk. I have so many gifts for you! You awakened late and rushed off to work. My tears were in the rain. Today you looked so sad – so all alone. It makes my heart ache because I understand. My friends set me down and hurt me many times too, but I love you. Oh, if you would only listen to me, I love you! I try to tell you in the blue sky and in the quiet green grass. I whisper it in the leaves on the trees and breathe in the colours of flowers. I shout it to you in mountain streams and give the birds love songs to sing. I clothe you with warm sunshine and perfume the air with nature scents. My love for you is deeper than the ocean and bigger than the biggest want or need in your head. Oh if you only knew how much I want to walk and talk with you. We could spend an eternity together in Heaven. I know how hard it is on this earth, I really know! I want to help you. I want you to meet my Father. He wants to help you too. My Father is that way, you know. Just call me – ask me – talk with me. Oh, please don't forget me. I have so much to share with you! Alright, I won't bother you any further. You are free to choose me. It is your decision. I have chosen you and because of this, I will wait because I love you.

Your Friend, Jesus.

MAYBE TOMORROW you could listen carefully for the ways in which God may be speaking to you. Could He also use you to speak to someone else through your words, emails, texts, or a loving act?

NIGHT PRAYER:

Speak, Lord! Your servant is listening. Amen.

BIBLE READING:

'Anyone with ears to hear must listen to the Spirit and understand what he is saying to the churches.' **Revelation 3:22, NLT**
The LORD Calls Samuel **1 Samuel 3:1–21**

FURTHER REFLECTION
BEING RECEPTIVE:

Master, speak! Though least and lowest,
Let me not unheard depart;
Master, speak! For O Thou knowest
All the yearning of my heart,
Knowest all its truest need;
Speak, and make me blest indeed.

Frances Ridley Havergal – English poet and hymn writer (1836–1879)

@daily_encourage

Look out for the little blessings in each day – especially tomorrow! ☺

Hannah Sarah Miles

SMILE:

I know that you believe that you understood what you think I said, but I am not sure you realise that what you heard is not what I meant.

Attributed to Robert J. McCloskey – US State Department spokesman at a briefing during the Vietnam War (1922–1996)

INNER BEAUTY

'There were a couple of unkempt homeless men rooting through a bin, trying to find food and rescue cardboard for their bedding.'

The prophet Samuel knew that Saul had been rejected by God and could no longer be the king of Israel. God had told him to go to the House of Jesse and anoint the next king. David was the youngest and least 'important' or 'significant' of Jesse's sons. His father almost forgot to call him in when Samuel came looking for a successor to Saul. Why? Because looking at him you wouldn't have thought he'd got it in him – he didn't look like the right material. Samuel had to ask if Jesse had any more sons, because the Lord had not chosen any of the seven sons that passed before him. Jesse thinks that surely his youngest, who was out tending the sheep, can't be the one! Yet he was called in – and the Bible tells us that he was the one to be chosen by God. Why? Because the Lord knew David's heart.

David was an accomplished musician. Samuel's first book tells how he soothed the troubled King Saul by playing his lyre. David, the shepherd, would've spent much of his time out on his own whilst looking after the sheep. But as he did that, he was praising the Lord, singing of the moon and the stars, the hills and the rivers. We know this because we have the benefit of reading the Psalms – a record of his songs and praises that probably became Jesus' hymnbook. David was the type of man that God wanted. He loved his Lord. God knew David was the right person to become king – no matter what he looked like.

When you're next reading the Psalms, think of that shepherd boy out on his own, but full of praise for the wonder of creation and the Creator who made it all. And while you're at it, think how the Saviour was born of the line of that same David. Jesus was to be the Good Shepherd who followed in the steps of His ancestor.

MAYBE TOMORROW you could ask yourself: am I more concerned with my outward appearance than my personal walk with the Lord? Who am I on the inside? (The ME that God loves so much.) Who am I when I'm alone? Does my devotional life make me attractive to God on the inside – despite any other shortcomings I may think I have? (Don't ever be tempted to think you are useless!) Do I judge others by their appearance?

NIGHT PRAYER:

As I prepare to sleep, I don't feel I'm very beautiful inside. Heavenly Father, You know what's been going on in my life today. Forgive me, in Jesus' name, and assure me of the plan You have for my life and that You know how You can use me – probably far more powerfully than I could ever believe or imagine. I know it won't necessarily be in dramatic ways, but still I know it can be life-changing for me and others. For Your kingdom's sake, I pray. Amen.

BIBLE READING:

'... The LORD does not look at the things people look at. People look at the outward appearance, but the LORD looks at the heart. **1 Samuel 16:7 (NIV, 2011)**
He had no beauty or majesty to attract us to him. **Isaiah 53**

FURTHER REFLECTION
BEING FAITHFUL TO WHO YOU ARE:

'I believe that God gives us our soul, our deepest identity, our True Self, our unique blueprint, at our own "immaculate conception". Our unique little bit of heaven is installed by the Manufacturer within the product, at the beginning! We are given a span of years to discover it, to choose it, and to live our destiny to the full.'

Richard Rohr – Franciscan friar and international speaker (1943–).
From Falling Upward[11]

@daily_encourage

God still loves us when our lives are a mess. He loves us when we don't act 'Christian'. God even loves us when we don't want Him to love us!

Hannah Sarah Miles

SMILE:

If plenty of sleep is an aid to good looks, it seems that a considerable number of people are suffering from insomnia.

Anon.

11 SMILE

'Frances gave me another perspective and corrected me with a smile ...'

Her little legs were swinging from side to side as she sat opposite me on the train. She was about five years old, with feet that couldn't reach the floor. She was looking around the carriage at commuters who were reading, sleeping, looking out of the window or deep in thought. She grinned, possibly at the sight of so many miserable and preoccupied people. Just then, she caught my eye – and I smiled at her smile. Her eyes brightened. She beamed and then looked away, slightly embarrassed. Then she peeped back to check I was still smiling.

As their stop arrived, her stressed mum closed her magazine and grabbed her daughter's arm without a word, dragging her towards the sliding doors. The little girl looked once more at all the people in the carriage, turned to me, smiled, gave me a secret wave, and was gone.

She left me grinning. Suddenly I began to realise just how miserable everyone else looked – which made me smile even more! As I smiled, one by one people curiously began to return the compliment. I was tempted to give them a secret wave too, but thought better of it.

MAYBE TOMORROW you could make someone's day with a smile. If you don't feel like smiling, then just imagine the smile of Jesus' love and Him giving you a secret, but knowing, wave. It may just help you rise above the mundane, and bring some hope and joy into your life. Smiles are contagious, so they can affect the lives of others. Mother Teresa once said, 'I will never understand all that a simple smile can accomplish.'

NIGHT PRAYER:

If I'm low tomorrow, Lord, send me an angel to brighten my day and to remind me of Your love. Then help me try to lift the spirits of those around me as I consider what makes YOU smile. Amen.

BIBLE READING:

'May the LORD smile on you and be gracious to you.'
Numbers 6:25, NLT
'When I smiled at them, they scarcely believed it; the light of my face was precious to them ...' **Job 29:21–25**

FURTHER REFLECTION
BEING A SMILER:

A SMILE
It costs nothing, but creates much.
It enriches those who receive, without impoverishing those who give.
It happens in a flash and the memory of it lasts forever.
None are so rich they can get along without it, and none so poor but are richer for its benefits.
It creates happiness in the home, fosters good will in a business, and is the countersign of friends.
It is rest to the weary, daylight to the discouraged, sunshine to the sad, and nature's best antidote for trouble.
Yet it cannot be bought, begged, borrowed, or stolen, for it is something that is no earthly good to anybody till it is given away!
If someone is too tired to give you a smile, leave one of yours.
For nobody needs a smile so much as those who have none to give.
Anon.

'The robbed that smiles, steals something from the thief.'

William Shakespeare – English playwright and poet (1564–1616). From Othello

@daily_encourage

'Every time you smile at someone, it is an action of love, a gift to that person, a beautiful thing.'

Mother Teresa

SMILE:

A laugh is a smile that bursts.

Mary H. Waldrip.

LITTLE THINGS MATTER

12

'We felt deeply for those who were going to be on the streets that night and resolved to do something to help the work of The Passage – a Christian organisation with a mission to help homeless people in Westminster.'

When I conduct funerals for bereaved families and prepare eulogies about loved ones, I'm conscious that it's typically the ordinary things about a person's character and habits that are remembered by family, friends and colleagues. What people have achieved, for example, isn't as significant as *who* people are, what their relationships were like, and how they treated others. Yet, when I pray, I tend to focus on the big decisions I am making in life, rather than the more mundane or less significant aspects of my daily routine.

I wonder what people will say about me when I pop my clogs. What will people really value? What will God value? Will I have paid enough attention to the little, but important, things in life? It seems to me that if I get who I am right in the ordinary and live well, my life will be enriched and so will the lives of others. Mother Teresa once said, 'We cannot do great things. We can only do small things with great love.'

MAYBE TOMORROW should be dedicated to doing little things well!

NIGHT PRAYER:

All-seeing God, forgive me that I do not always do 'small things with great love'. I feel a hypocrite at times, better in a crisis, but inconsistent when it comes to daily living. One moment I get it right, and then any good I've done seems cancelled out by my thoughtlessness or selfishness. Help me to be faithful in *all* things – authentic, honest, loving and forgiving. Most of all, help me not to hurt those I love the most, but to show them just how much they mean to me. I ask this in Jesus' name. Amen.

BIBLE READING:

Jesus said, 'Whoever can be trusted with very little can also be trusted with much, and whoever is dishonest with very little will also be dishonest with much.' **Luke 16:10**
Martha and Mary **Luke 10:38–42**

FURTHER REFLECTION
BEING FRUITFUL:

Where's this day gone, Lord?
There were so many things I meant to do but
my best intentions haven't come to much.
Maybe if I make a list, tomorrow I'll do better.
And maybe, just putting things on paper will
confront me with what is truly important and
worthwhile, and what is time-wasting and
selfish. You inspired the great apostle
Paul to write a list of spiritual 'fruits' for new
Christians. Maybe tomorrow, Lord, that will
be the first list to inspire me. So, I'm just
going to pray now, Lord Jesus Christ, help
me to live by Love, Joy, Peace, Patience,
Kindness, Goodness, Faithfulness,
Gentleness and Self-control. Amen.

@daily_encourage

Don't give up on God because He will NEVER give up on you!

Hannah Sarah Miles

SMILE:

A man wanted a boat more than anything. His wife kept refusing, but he bought one anyway. 'I'll tell you what,' he told her. 'In the spirit of compromise, why don't you name the boat?' Being a good sport, she accepted. When her husband went to the dock for his maiden voyage, this is the name he saw painted on the side: 'For Sale'.

Anon.

13 LOST AND LONELY

'Yes, we'd both had a challenging day, but at least we had eaten and were returning to the warmth and security of our home and the company of family.'

Frances and I took a short trip to Durham and enjoyed walking around and visiting the Cathedral. It was a refreshing break, which sadly came to an end all too soon. We had booked a taxi to take us to the station for the trip home. En route, the driver told us about an overseas student who'd recently booked a ride with him. The passenger knew very little English, but asked to be picked up from the city centre. The taxi firm needed his exact location. The student couldn't say where he was, so he was asked to read out a road name from a nearby sign. He looked around and replied, *'Give Way'*!

You'll be glad to know the student and taxi driver did eventually find each other and reached their destination.

It made me realise that, while Frances and I were enjoying each other's company, there were plenty of others close by who would be feeling lost, alone and vulnerable: maybe visitors, refugees or asylum seekers; or those just out of prison, homeless people, or members of the 'awkward brigade' that people avoid; or perhaps those who are single, bereaved, or just plain isolated and lonely.

MAYBE TOMORROW you could – like the sign said – 'give way' to some of your busyness and pause to pray for those who may be feeling 'out of it'. Or, better still, is there anyone you could befriend or spend time with in the coming day? Even in a crowd, there may be lonely people.

'Loneliness is the first thing which God's eye named, not good.'
John Milton – English Poet (1608–1674)

NIGHT PRAYER:

When I feel very alone, Lord, may Your Holy Spirit be my Comforter and enable me to rest conscious of Your love. When I rise, may I find someone whose loneliness I can ease, that together we may find company, hope and direction for our lives. Amen.

BIBLE READING:

Jesus said, ... 'And surely I am with you always, to the very end of the age.' **Matthew 28:20b**
Jesus' Friends **John 15:13–15**

FURTHER REFLECTION
BEING NEVER ALONE:

As He threw stars into the sky, moulded the earth, lit the sun and created you,
so, also, will God show you the plans and purpose that He has for your life.
Be still and listen, for no matter how many problems you may have,
how troubled you are or how alone you feel,
He is at your side with a loving hand on your shoulder.
As you weep so, too, does He.

In the silence of the night He will be there,
in the rush and noise of traffic He will be there,
in your tears of sadness He will be there
– always His hand will be upon your shoulder.
Such is the enormity, grace and love of God.

Used with permission. Copyright © Derek Dobson 2009 www.reflectionsofhope.org

@daily_encourage

Even when you're walking on an invisible sidewalk, God says two words: 'Trust Me.'

Hannah Sarah Miles

SMILE:

Bring all your old newspapers – and your neighbours too. Please tie them up.

A Cornish church bulletin Blooper – Anon.

WORRY

14

'Despite worries and stresses of her own, she had dashed up to London for a church meeting.'

Frances Miles writes: The phone call was short and to the point, 'Mum, Dad ... it's me. The satnav took me towards London and I've been driving for ages but I am lost. What do I do?' It was nearly midnight. Our 18-year-old had gone to visit a friend for the evening and was now trying to get back. There's nothing like a call from your child late at night to keep you awake – until you hear the car, and daughter, arriving safely back home! But I find it's not just the dramatic stuff that can stop me from sleeping. Perhaps it's a 'female' thing; sometimes I wonder if we worry more than men. There is often so much swilling around my head that it's hard to let go. Keeping a pen and paper handy to make a list of things that need to be done the next day is useful, but so is the practice of giving thanks to God for the day that is past, giving Him the names of the people who are on my heart, and any concerns about the day that lies ahead.

'Sleep sound in Jesus' was a music tape of soothing lullabies we played to our daughter when she was a baby as we drove her around in the car. It certainly did the job! Perhaps tonight I can lay down my cares, worries and 'to do' lists, and simply sleep soundly in Jesus' love.

MAYBE TOMORROW you will be refreshed and ready to face the new day too ... worry free.

NIGHT PRAYER:

Lord, I am sorry when I forget You are here with me. Forgive my foolish stressing and worrying about everything and let me simply give it to You. For You want me to unburden my heart, because in some incredible and inexplicable way, You can take on everybody's concerns – without stressing. What an amazing God! Amen.

Used with permission. Copyright © Frances H. Miles January 2012

BIBLE READING:

'Cast all your anxiety on him because he cares for you.' **1 Peter 5:7**
Do not worry about tomorrow **Matthew 6:25–34**

FURTHER REFLECTION
BEING IN NEED OF ASSURANCE:

Don't leave me Lord; I am often overwhelmed with responsibilities, all craving my attention,
many demands – all jostling for priority. I need You beside me.
Don't leave me Lord; I don't feel confident to do all You ask of me. To be honest I have had to leave too many loose ends today. I need Your assurance.
Don't leave me Lord; I know You wouldn't ask of me anything that was beyond me,
but I'm exhausted and feel worn out. I need Your strength.
Lord, help me to know Your presence with me in my darkest moments of desolation and despair
and when I feel anxious, lonely and insecure.
Please help me to live differently tomorrow. Give me Your assurance that You are always with me.
Encourage me to dig deep into the limitless resources of Your grace and truth
so I may walk with renewed confidence and know the certainty that You are there beside me
and will never leave me or forsake me. Thank You Lord!

Used with permission. Copyright © John Izzard November 2011

@daily_encourage

Anything that is bothering you today, no matter how small it may feel, God wants to hear it. He wants to replace your fears with joy & peace.

Hannah Sarah Miles

SMILE:

Tom had been a compulsive worrier for years until he found a way to overcome this problem. His friends noticed the dramatic change. 'You don't seem to be worried about anything anymore.' 'I hired a professional worrier for a thousand pounds a week,' Tom replied, 'I haven't had a single qualm since.' 'A thousand a week!' said Doug. 'How are you going to pay him?' 'That's his problem!'

Anon.

BEING ON A ROLLER-COASTER

THE ROLLER-COASTER PRAYER

Lord Jesus,
When life is like a roller-coaster,
With the earth no longer below or the sky above.
When north is south and east is west,
And all the familiar landmarks of my security are gone ...
Will you be for me my one unshakeable place,
My one immovable point of focus,
My rock that doesn't roll?
After all – you are the alpha and omega,
Beginning and end ...
So come share the ride with me,
And turn the screams of fear
Into victorious shouts of praise! AMEN!

Written in October 2007 by my friend and encourager,
Rob Frost, in the weeks before he died.
Used with Jacqui's kind permission.
Copyright © Revd Dr Rob Frost (1950–2007)

LOVING AND SERVING

All heroic lives remind us
We can make our lives sublime,
And, departing, leave behind us
Footprints on the sands of time;
Footprints that perhaps another,
Sailing o'er life's solemn main,
Forlorn sister or lost brother,
Seeing, shall take heart again.

Let us then be up and doing,
With a heart for any fate;
Still achieving, still pursuing,
Learn to labour and to wait.
Not enjoyment, and not sorrow,
Is our destined end or way;
But to act that each tomorrow
Finds us further than today.

Henry Wadsworth Longfellow – American professor, linguist, and poet (1807–1882)

15 A PERTINENT QUESTION

'Eventually a delicious and fairly extravagant meal arrived and we were just about to tuck in when we saw a disturbing sight just outside the window.'

One cold wet day in London the Miles family was seeking a restaurant for warmth and food. All of a sudden my then six-year-old daughter, Hannah, saw three homeless men wrapped in sleeping bags and sheltering from the weather. Sadly, this isn't an uncommon sight, but it was new to my children. We were just about to walk past to get out of the rain, when Hannah and her younger brother, Jonathan, put the brakes on and brought us to a halt. 'What are they doing, Mummy?' asked Hannah. 'Why are they there, Dad?' Then in a loud voice for all to hear, Jonathan said, 'Are they poor?'

Well, Mum and Dad were just about to find a sympathetic and helpful explanation, when Hannah fired more questions: 'What can we do? Can't we have them come and stay with us?' Jonathan added, 'Please can we give them some money?' I have to admit, I wasn't going to stop, but we did. We gave our children a few measly coins and they went over to the rough-looking men, who appeared moved by their gesture.

This new Good Samaritan story haunted me, the minister who was going to 'walk by on the other side'. Yes, it was reasonable to want to protect my children, yet through them God spoke to me. In them I saw and felt the purity of unconditional love. I was moved by their distress at the reality of homelessness and their surprise at *my* hardness of heart. As I went on to eat my burger and fries, I could hear Jesus saying to me: '... I tell you the truth, whatever you did for one of the least of these brothers of mine, you did for me' (Matt. 25:40). Lord, forgive me!

MAYBE TOMORROW you can refuse to get used to homelessness. In the face of poverty, never stop asking 'Why are they there?' That is, until Hannah's question no longer needs to be asked.

NIGHT PRAYER:

Lord of the friendless, You spent time with those in need. You command me to love my neighbour as myself – regardless of who that may be. Melt my hardened heart and give me wisdom to know how I can best serve my sisters and brothers in Your name. Amen.[12]

BIBLE READING:

'"The most important [commandment]," answered Jesus, "is this: 'Hear, O Israel: The Lord our God, the Lord is one. Love the Lord your God with all your heart and with all your soul and with all your mind and with all your strength.' The second is this: 'Love your neighbour as yourself.' There is no commandment greater than these."' **Mark 12:29–31** The Good Samaritan **Luke 10:25–37**

FURTHER REFLECTION
BEING A BARRIER BREAKER:

Father, we thank you that Jesus came to break down barriers.
He did not see the migrant or the settled,
the housed or the homeless, the employed or the unemployed;
He saw and loved the person.
Forgive us when we put up barriers between ourselves and others;
help us show love to all without constraint.
Help us, your church, to build communities without barriers,
where all are valued because all are made in your image.
In Jesus' name. Amen.

*Used with permission. Copyright © Poverty and Homelessness Action Week
partnership 2012 www.actionweek.org.uk*

@daily_encourage

Pray that we may see people as God sees them, not by face,
but by heart.

Hannah Sarah Miles

SMILE:

A homeless man asked me for £5 for a cup of tea. 'What?' I
replied, 'A mug of tea doesn't cost a fiver!' 'You're quite right,'
came the reply, 'I'm just a big tipper!'

Anon.

A CHEERFUL GIVER 16

'... it might be a way of highlighting the plight of homelessness and raising a little bit of money in the process.'

Aged just six years old, Caitlin was an early and avid reader. She read Louisa May Alcott's book *Little Women* and was inspired by one of the characters, Jo, who cuts her hair and sells it so her mother has money to visit her sick father. So Caitlin decided to grow her hair and donate it to help a child with cancer. She did this secretly, determined to help make a wig for a child suffering the effects of chemotherapy. She told those who asked why she'd done it, 'It's not nice to be stared at and I felt I could help.' Two years later, after persevering with knots and tangles, Caitlin's hair had grown long enough to be cut. By then she'd told her friends and it inspired them to get involved too. She said, 'I think it's really nice that my classmates were interested and wanted to sponsor me. They gave up their pocket money to help.'

The great Hair Cut took place just before Christmas one year, and even the local mayor came to support her. Afterwards her locks were given to the wigmakers. When asked what she'd learnt, Caitlin replied, 'Doing something little can help someone in a big way. It doesn't matter whether or not they know it's you that helped. It just makes you feel good about yourself. I feel great!' I guess it was tough for Caitlin every time she brushed those tangles. Giving generously and compassionately isn't always easy, but the surprising thing is it can bring great joy.

MAYBE TOMORROW is a day for remembering that costly giving is at the heart of Christianity, 'For God loved the world so much he gave his only Son …' – Jesus.

NIGHT PRAYER:

Lord Jesus, You taught that unless I become like a little child, I will
never understand Your kingdom of love. Thank You that Caitlin
has reminded me what giving is all about. Help me never to be too
proud to learn from the purity and innocence of children. Amen.

BIBLE READING:

'And [Jesus] said: "I tell you the truth, unless you change and
become like little children, you will never enter the kingdom of
heaven."' **Matthew 18:3**
For God so loved the world **John 3:16–21**

FURTHER REFLECTION
BEING GENEROUS:

They were homeless, and living on the street outside my flat.
I wanted them removed. 'Helped' or even 'housed' never
entered my mind. 'Loved' was not even a distant thought.
I remember the morning vividly.

It was cold, but my heart was far colder than the air. At that
moment I sensed the Lord's overwhelming and unconditional
love. I knew He loved me despite my feelings and I knew He
was calling me to love my neighbour. Since that day I've spent
a lot of time with people who have been homeless. I've heard
some pretty horrific stories of abuse, neglect, guilt and shame.
But I'm still astounded when someone thanks me for simply
holding their hand. Those living on the streets are often
stepped over and ignored. Unable to bathe, they go untouched.
Being generous takes many forms, but the simple act of
holding a hand costs nothing. Maybe tomorrow, consider
that generosity takes many forms. It may be a financial gift
to a homeless shelter, giving away your sandwich, or simply
stopping to listen … and holding a hand.

Used with permission. Copyright © Michael O'Neill October 2011
www.stewardship.org.uk

@daily_encourage

'May the LORD repay you for what you have done. May you be richly rewarded by the LORD ...' (Ruth 2:12).

Hannah Sarah Miles

SMILE:

When it comes to giving, some people stop at nothing.

Anon.

Do yer givin', while yer livin', so you'll be knowin' where it's goin.

Anon.

17 SOME THINGS TAKE TIME AND EFFORT

'… Some things take time.'

When younger, my children embarrassingly named our cat 'Pixie'. At night you'll find me calling her name from the back door, trying to get her inside. I'm sure my neighbours think I'm looking for fairies at the bottom of our garden. Pixie was a rescue cat and for years was frightened of adults, but she was very affectionate with the children. Sadly, she regarded any grown-up with suspicion – even those who were gentle and caring towards her. Apart from a little bit of 'cupboard love', I knew she didn't really trust me. Then a miracle happened after about seven years of Pixie being in our home: she jumped onto my lap! I'm not sure whether she wasn't thinking straight and got the wrong person, but she stayed there for ages and I didn't have the heart to move. It didn't happen again for a while, but I think she must have realised I wasn't so bad after all. She had taken her time, but trust had been built and a new relationship was possible. Gradually she became more friendly and confident towards me, Frances, and occasionally other visitors too. Now whenever I watch the late evening news, she rushes over and will cuddle up for about half an hour – it's about the only regular time I sit still long enough. It's therapeutic and calming listening to her purring. I'm sure she smiles too.

MAYBE TOMORROW you could be more patient with relationships, remembering they can take time to nurture or heal – especially if there are past hurts or other 'history' leading to suspicion, prejudice, or unease. Relationships have to be worked at carefully, prayerfully and hopefully. It is costly, but worth it.

NIGHT PRAYER:

I'm sorry, Lord. I'm often impatient and self-centred. There are times when I love only when I know it will be returned. May I be a good neighbour tomorrow and enjoy offering random acts of kindness. Amen.

BIBLE READING:

'Be kind and compassionate to one another, forgiving each other, just as in Christ God forgave you.' **Ephesians 4:32**
Bless those who persecute you **Romans 12:9–21**

FURTHER REFLECTION
BEING SALT:

Lord, thank you for the kindness of an anonymous neighbour who thoughtfully sprinkled salt on the pavement on a winter morning. The salt reminded me of your thoughts for me.
SALT.
Strong enough to take on the early morning ice and prevent an inevitable slip.
Confident to stay where it was placed and to have an impact without creating a mess ... or a fuss.
Safe enough not to need a warning sign, and already having an impact when I encountered it.
Impartial enough to keep making a difference for whoever comes around the corner.

Lord, you invite me to be salty too.
Strong enough to think of my neighbour.
Confident enough to make a difference for my neighbour.
Safe enough to be with my neighbour.

Impartial enough to be welcoming to my neighbour.

Let your thoughts towards me and your presence in me
overflow in thoughtful acts of kindness, too. Amen.

Used with permission. Copyright © Katei Kirby November 2011

@daily_encourage

Challenge: be completely & totally honest with someone.
Tell them how you feel about something. Even if it requires
you to be vulnerable!

Hannah Sarah Miles

SMILE:

I am extraordinarily patient, provided I get my way in the end.

*Baroness Margaret Thatcher (1925–) British Prime Minister 1979–1990,
the Observer, 4 April 1989.*

MAKING A DIFFERENCE

18

'It would be good to try and make a difference.'

I sometimes despair that life is so hard on the poor, suffering and persecuted of the world – especially after watching the evening news. This planet is such a complicated place and its people can be so cruel. I ask myself, 'What difference have I made today?' If I'm honest, I often feel guilty that my life is privileged and comfortable; my trials and traumas pale into insignificance in comparison to many. Yet, I'm slowly learning that there are small things I can do that, if offered to God, He can use to do amazing things.

I always encourage people to exercise their right to vote in elections. 'But what difference will it make?' is often the reply. Well, if everyone were apathetic we'd have no one elected or, even worse, unsuitable people in power by default. We may not vote for the successful candidate, but our vote will have counted. Just look at those who win elections by narrow margins. You may think you're insignificant, but you're not. You *can* make a difference in this world – especially when you pray for guidance and the help of the Holy Spirit.

MAYBE TOMORROW can be a 'make-a-difference day'. You may not feel that you're a 'mover and a shaker', but God is, and He can work through even you to further His kingdom. Trust Him and never underestimate the difference that you can make if you pray, listen, and act!

NIGHT PRAYER:

God of Justice and Change, water and nourish the seed
of my faith, that I may bear fruit for You. Forgive me for
underestimating my influence. Use me tomorrow to further
Your kingdom … bit by bit. Amen.

BIBLE READING:

'For we are God's workmanship, created in Christ Jesus to
do good works, which God prepared in advance for us to do.'
Ephesians 2:10
Faith and deeds **James 2:14–25**

FURTHER REFLECTION
BEING AN AGENT OF TRANSFORMATION:

One song can spark a moment,
One flower can wake the dream.
One tree can start a forest,
One bird can herald spring.
One smile begins a friendship,
One handclasp lifts a soul.
One star can guide a ship at sea,
One word can frame the goal.
One vote can change a nation,
One sunbeam lights a room.
One candle wipes out darkness,
One laugh will conquer gloom.
One step must start each journey,
One word must start each prayer.
One hope will raise our spirits,
One touch can show you care.
One voice can speak with wisdom,
One heart can know what's true,
One life can make the difference.
You see, *it's up to you!*
Anon.

@daily_encourage

Break my heart for what breaks Yours today, Lord.

Hannah Sarah Miles

SMILE:

I don't know, I don't care, and it doesn't make any difference!

Albert Einstein – German-born American physicist (1879–1955)

19 SPREAD THE LOVE

'*... had we become self-centred and numb to the need that was
staring us in the face?*'

'Why have you put cheese on the table for breakfast?' asked my
daughter (aged six at the time). The 'cheese' was in fact butter
that we'd bought as a treat because we had visitors. They teased
us that our 'poor deprived children' were obviously only used to
margarine. Yet, if we had been more used to butter we would've
taken it out of the fridge earlier or bought spreadable butter.
There was more hilarity because it was too hard to spread.

Hearts can sometimes become cold and hard too – and I'm
not talking about our visitors. There are times when I can get
tired of giving my time, or I become cynical, or even suffer from
what's been called 'compassion fatigue'. This often happens
when I'm weary, or stressed, and I haven't kept close to my
heavenly Father. It is the Holy Spirit who can warm a cold heart.
John Wesley talked about having his heart 'strangely warmed'
when he put his trust in Christ. He was filled with God's love
and a passion to share the good news with everyone. He strived
to walk the talk and to be perfect in love. Mother Teresa once
said, 'Spread love everywhere you go: first of all in your own
house. Give love to your children, to your wife or husband,
to a next-door neighbour ... Let no one ever come to you
without leaving better and happier. Be the living expression of
God's kindness; kindness in your face, kindness in your eyes,
kindness in your smile, kindness in your warm greeting.'

MAYBE TOMORROW you can pray that you'll be warm-
hearted, so you can 'spread the love' wherever you go.

NIGHT PRAYER:

Love divine, all loves excelling,
Joy of heaven, to earth come down;
Fix in us thy humble dwelling;
All thy faithful mercies crown!
Jesus, Thou art all compassion,
Pure unbounded love Thou art;
Visit us with Thy salvation;
Enter every trembling heart.

Charles Wesley – hymn writer, poet, evangelist and co-founder of the Methodist movement with his brother John (1707–1788)

BIBLE READING:

St Paul said, 'Do everything in love.' **1 Corinthians 16:14**
God's love and ours **1 John 4:7–21**

FURTHER REFLECTION
BEING LOVING:

Love is patient, love is kind, it has no enemies
It perseveres in the face of adversity – it never gives up
Love listens, understands and consoles
Love does not run away when unhappiness knocks on the door
It will stand and fight for that which is right
Love knows no nationality, it has no flag, no anthem, yet it is shared by all
Love will support, encourage and inspire
It is not vain or boastful save in God
Were it not for love, life would cease to have meaning
Love will protect those most dear and always show compassion
It is in loving and forgiving that people are healed.

Based on 1 Corinthians 13. Used with permission. Copyright © Derek Dobson 2011 www.reflectionsofhope.org

@daily_encourage

When faced with the impossible, just trust, wait and expect
Him to work. The impossible is His forte!

Hannah Sarah Miles

SMILE:

If love is the answer, could you rephrase the question?

Lily Tomlin – American actress, comedienne, writer and producer (1939–)

GOD NEVER FINISHES WITH US! 20

'I felt terribly guilty I hadn't really spent enough time with God, my colleagues, or those I love.'

I used to be able to remember names. I now have 'senior moments' and even occasionally forget the names of those I know well. As I approach 50, I also find text is much smaller these days. I have to hold labels further away to read them. And am I alone in climbing the stairs, only to forget what I went up for? Very frustrating! As someone rightly said, 'Everybody wants to live a long time, but nobody wants to get old.' I can only begin to imagine what it's like when such experiences get worse with age. It's sobering to think that one in six people over 80 has a form of dementia – and many know they have it, too.

In the West, old age is often unappreciated and ridiculed, rather than respected as it is in many cultures. As people live longer, we can't ignore how crucial it is that we respect and value age. It's biblical too: 'Rise in the presence of the aged, show respect for the elderly and revere your God ...' (Lev. 19:32). Someone said, 'Sixty-five is the age when one acquires sufficient experience to lose one's job!' Well, others may pension people off, but God never finishes with us. Remember Anna in the Bible? She was an 84-year-old widow who'd known sorrow, yet she hadn't grown bitter. Anna remained hopeful and never ceased to worship or pray. What's more, God made use of her faith, righteousness and wisdom.

MAYBE TOMORROW you could spend time with an elderly neighbour, or speak to a relative you've neglected. Remember too, that with care, those with dementia can thrive, and they have gifts they can offer us all.

TM

NIGHT PRAYER (FOR AN OLDER PERSON):

Thank you Lord, for your goodness all the years of my life.
Looking back gives a different perspective
and I can see your hand on everything.
I can see how you worked things out; I see so many Romans 8:28s!
Thank you for showing me that, Lord,
because I need more of you now, than ever.
I never knew being old would be like this.
I never knew it would be such a battle,
But thank you, Father, you haven't changed.
You've brought me thus far, and you will bring me Home.
Amen.

Used with permission. Copyright © Louise Morse August 2011
www.pilgrimsfriend.org.uk

BIBLE READING:

'And we know that in all things God works for the good of those who love him, who have been called according to his purpose.' **Romans 8:28**
Simeon and Anna **Luke 2:25–38**

FURTHER REFLECTION
BEING A CARER FOR A LOVED ONE WITH DEMENTIA:

Lord, I hardly know how to begin ....
Sometimes weariness just rolls over me and I sink into despair.
At times it feels we've been plunged into such darkness
That I can't see *her (him)* at all. The person I love – gone.

Yet, you've said that the darkness cannot hide us from you,
You see us as clearly as if all were light.
Father, please give me your eyes to see,
Your ears to hear and your strength to carry on.
May your Spirit within me touch the spirit within *her (him)*
and bring comfort and peace;
and quicken that foretaste of eternity, so that we know there is
more than this. Amen.

Used with permission. Copyright © Louise Morse August 2011
www.pilgrimsfriend.org.uk

@daily_encourage

You are never too old and you are never too young to do
something impactful and awesome for God!

Hannah Sarah Miles

SMILE:

Everyone has birthdays ... even grandads!

Hannah Sarah Miles – aged four

21 THE WISE CONSUMER

'… we were able to watch the world going by as we sipped our drinks and waited for our food.'

Andrew Graystone writes: Nowadays most of us are very conscious of the food we eat. We buy eggs that are free-range, coffee that has been fairly-traded and bananas that send postcards home to their mothers. We read the labels on the packets. We want to know about nutritional content. We want to know that the animals that we eat were treated well. We care about who produced the food and whether they were paid a fair price for their work. We care about these things because we care about our own health and that of our children. And that's great. We also care because buying food that is produced justly with the minimum harm to the environment is an important part of our Christian discipleship. And that's even better.

Quite rightly we care about what we put in our mouths. But we're often completely blasé about what we put in our minds. TV, radio, magazines and newspapers can feed our thoughts and our prayers.

MAYBE TOMORROW it is worth remembering that junk media is as bad for the soul as junk food for the body.

NIGHT PRAYER:

God of grace, I have seen so much today;
TV programmes, adverts, news stories and logos fill my mind.
I think I have media indigestion.
As I sleep, please sift and sort the images of my day,
And help me to choose carefully what I look at tomorrow.
Amen.

Used with permission. Copyright © Andrew Graystone 2011 www.churchandmedia.net

BIBLE READING:

'… whatever is true, whatever is noble, whatever is right,
whatever is pure, whatever is lovely, whatever is admirable –
if anything is excellent or praiseworthy – think about such
things.' **Philippians 4:8**
'Do not love the world or anything in the world. If anyone loves
the world, the love of the Father is not in him …' **1 John 2:15–17**

FURTHER REFLECTION
BEING A PERSON OF INTEGRITY:

Lord, today I am reminded of what is missing in me,
The bare branches where fruit should be.
But I know Your grace is sufficient.
Tomorrow, help me live more truly
Walking in paths of integrity
For Your name's sake. Amen.

Used with permission. Copyright © Elizabeth Hunter October 2011
www.theosthinktank.co.uk

@daily_encourage

I want to encourage you to analyse your heart. God wants you to be faithful to the calling He has given, which is ultimately for His glory.

Hannah Sarah Miles

SMILE:

'I watch about six hours of TV a day. Seven if there's something good on.'

Bart Simpson – from the animated television series The Simpsons

BEING MINDFUL OF THOSE IN PRISON

Out of sight! Out of mind?

I relax in my easy chair, watching television, ready for my comfortable bed.
But for those in prison, a hard chair in a tiny cell, and a bed with a thin, bumpy mattress.

Time for my bedtime drink – tea, cocoa, or perhaps some wine, and favourite snacks?
But for the prisoner, hot water, a tea bag in a plastic mug and maybe a few biscuits.

Still time to make one more phone call and send some emails.
But in prison, 'lock up' was at 6.30pm – alone until morning apart from the night-shift officer's face at the hatch.

I feel secure at home with family; and we have good neighbours.
But the prisoner – surrounded by 800 strangers, just crime and conviction in common.

Relishing tomorrow – a new work project, badminton and a meal with friends!
But for prisoners, monotony. Tomorrow will be like yesterday, and the day before, and …

Used with permission. Copyright © Revd Gordon Newton September 2011

TRIALS AND TRAUMAS

TOMORROW

Clouds fill the sky;
Your life darkens and the world disappears;
Everything becomes totally meaningless.
– But, as with time, the clouds pass and
reveal the sun which was there all the time.

As you look into the sunlight, your face
shines again whilst your shadow appears behind you.
The future beckons as you hold out a
nervous and shaking hand.
One step at a time
– One day at a time
Slowly but surely your strength will grow
and slowly but surely life will grow.

There was a time when every day seemed like yesterday
But there will come a time when today greets tomorrow;
When your mirror becomes a window;
It is then that you will see your future
and not reflect on the past.

Have Faith, have Courage and have Hope
for you **will** survive.[13]

Used with permission. Copyright © Derek Dobson 1998 www.reflectionsofhope.org

WHEN THE WORLD'S ON YOUR SHOULDERS

22

I love A.A. Milne's *Winnie the Pooh*. I'm something of a Tigger character myself, but do you remember Rabbit? There was one very busy day when 'as soon as he woke up he felt important, as if everything depended on him'. A 'Captainish sort of day'. Well, there are times when I can really identify with Rabbit – especially when I'm feeling the weight of responsibility, or tempted to believe I'm indispensible.

Do you have days when people's expectations seem to outweigh your ability to cope? Did the world seem to be on your shoulders today? Whatever your gifts or personality, it's important to speak and act as though everything depends on *God* and not you. That doesn't mean shirking your responsibilities, but allowing Christ to work in and through you in every situation. It also means getting things into perspective and not thinking you're all-important or believing the world will fall apart without you.

MAYBE TOMORROW is a day for being less self-reliant! Why not share your burdens with others? Lean on God too and tell Him your concerns. Then, in humility, surrender your circumstances to the One who loves you and let Him work in your life. At a time of persecution the apostle Peter wrote: 'If anyone speaks, he should do it as one speaking the very words of God. If anyone serves, he should do it with the strength God provides ...' (1 Pet. 4:11). He mentions two distinct roles: speaking God's Word and then serving. Both are needed, but they should be God's gracious work in

Christians – He alone gives the inspiration, strength, and blessing that's needed.

NIGHT PRAYER

Lord Jesus, may Your Spirit enable me to live and speak for my Father tomorrow. To Him be the glory and the power for ever and ever. Amen.

BIBLE READING:

Paul said, 'For by the grace given me I say to every one of you: do not think of yourself more highly than you ought, but rather think of yourself with sober judgment, in accordance with the faith God has given you.' **Romans 12:3**
Living for God **1 Peter 4:1–11**

FURTHER REFLECTION
BEING AT WORK WITH GOD:

Work shall be prayer, if all be wrought
As Thou wouldst have it done,
And prayer, by Thee inspired and taught,
Itself with work be one.

John Ellerton – hymn writer and hymnologist (1826–1893)

Forth in thy name, O Lord, I go,
My daily labour to pursue,
Thee, only thee, resolved to know
In all I think, or speak, or do.

Charles Wesley – hymn writer, poet, evangelist and co-founder of the Methodist movement with his brother, John (1707–1788)

@daily_encourage

Hold tight to your God-given dreams. He will not let you down!

Hannah Sarah Miles

SMILE:

What is wrong with everyone nowadays? Why do they all seem to think they are qualified to do things far beyond their actual capabilities?

Prince Charles – Prince of Wales (1948–)

Pray as though everything depended on God. Work as though everything depended on you.

St Augustine of Hippo – influential Christian thinker, philosopher/theologian (354–430)

23 INTERRUPTIONS

Will I ever get this thought written? Each time I've made a start something has happened. The phone rang, someone called at the door, I received a text message, and emails kept pinging as they arrived demanding attention – as if there's nothing else to do but respond instantly! I'm slowly learning to switch email off, put the mobile on silent, focus on just one thing at a time, and try to rein in my tendency to multi-task. Yet, despite my best efforts, frustrating disruptions can still come. This leaves my 'To Do' list as long at the end of the day as it was at the beginning.

Whilst it's important to address what the author Tony Schwartz calls my 'poverty of attention',[14] it's interesting how sometimes unexpected and irritating nuisances can turn out to be important. Scheduled tasks may get delayed, but some interruptions end up being the real business of the day.

You'll be glad to know this sort of thing happened to Jesus too. You may remember His conversation with a rich young man. The Lord had been teaching the crowds, but the time came for Him to leave the house where He was staying to head for Jerusalem. Mark tells us that an interruption came as Jesus 'started on his way' (Mark 10:17). Then Luke points out that it was a 'young synagogue ruler' who eagerly approached the Lord, fell at His feet, addressed Him respectfully as 'good teacher', and then posed a question. Jesus could've said, 'Sorry, not now, I'm busy and I've got to go.' But He didn't. Instead, He gave His time and attention and the interruption prompted some significant and challenging teaching for all those listening.

MAYBE TOMORROW is a day to bear in mind that, despite being focused, Jesus had time for certain disruptions. He had time for people – and not only the worthy, rich and powerful. In the day ahead, remember that Jesus is never too busy to hear the concerns of your heart. He can also use you and me, if we seek to imitate Him when we are interrupted – despite our frustrations at what can seem a 'pain in the neck' at the time.

NIGHT PRAYER:

All-knowing and compassionate Lord, speak to me tomorrow through the unexpected, as well as my best-laid plans. Amen.

BIBLE READING:

'[The Lord] will reply, "Truly I tell you, whatever you did not do for one of the least of these, you did not do for me."'
Matthew 25:45 (NIV, 2011)
The rich and the kingdom of God **Mark 10:17–31**

FURTHER REFLECTION
BEING INTERRUPTIBLE:

Prepare me, Lord,
for when You knock on my door tomorrow.
May I not be resentful or unaware of Your visit,
but help me give myself in love to friend and stranger as You have commanded.
When my comfortable routine is interrupted,
may I discern the whisper of Your Spirit
and find Your will for my life in work, devotion and even in leisure.
When I am tired and need space,
guide me to the place of refreshment and renewal
that You have prepared for me and those that I love dearly.
Thank You, Lord. Amen.
TM

@daily_encourage

God does not see you as a failure. You learn more from failure.
God sees you as a learner.

Hannah Sarah Miles

SMILE:

The church chapel is open 24 hours a day. Please use the
chapel during those hours *only*.

Blooper – Anon.

APPROPRIATE TIME 24

Riding on the London Underground is an occupational hazard when you work in Westminster. I'm frequently amused that the digital display on the platform tells me with authority that my train will arrive in, say, three minutes. It's my experience that those three minutes are not always made up of three lots of 60 seconds. The train arrives when it can. On one occasion my train was delayed because someone went into labour and held everything up. How inconvenient ... especially for the woman concerned! She certainly had my prayers.

Now, I'm sure the newborn didn't arrive exactly nine months on from conception, but when the baby was ready. There's a difference between chronological time and appropriate time. In one of his letters, Saint Paul writes: 'But when the time had fully come, God sent his Son, born of a woman, born under law, to redeem those under law, that we might receive the full rights of sons' (Gal. 4:4). In other words, God sent His Son, Jesus, when the time was right.

MAYBE TOMORROW is a day for remembering that God doesn't wear a watch and isn't bound by time or a calendar. God acts when the time is right. So, if you're waiting for prayers to be answered, or wondering why God seems to take His time over things, then be encouraged: God will act according to His perfect will, when the time is appropriate. Remember too, that He is Maker of time and Creator of all that is and views things from the perspective of eternity.

NIGHT PRAYER:

All-knowing God, grant me patience and trust that You will answer my prayers, not as I ask in my ignorance, nor as I deserve in my sinfulness, but as You know and love me through Jesus Christ, my Lord. Amen.

BIBLE READING:

'There is a time for everything, and a season for every activity under heaven ...' **Ecclesiastes 3:1**
Jesus waits for the right time **John 7:1–13**

FURTHER REFLECTION
BEING PATIENT AND AT PEACE:

'Have patience with all things,
But, first of all with yourself.'
St Francis de Sales

'Do not look forward to what might happen tomorrow. The same everlasting Father who cares for you today will take care of you tomorrow and every day. Either He will shield you from suffering or He will give you unfailing strength to bear it. Be at peace then and put aside all anxious thoughts and imaginations.'

St Francis de Sales
Roman Catholic Saint and Bishop of Geneva (1567–1622)

@daily_encourage

Just because things didn't go the way we planned, doesn't mean things haven't gone the way He planned. Keep trusting!!

Hannah Sarah Miles

SMILE:

A visiting preacher was very long-winded. What was worse, every time he would make a good point during his sermon and a member of the congregation responded with 'Amen' or 'That's right, preacher', he would get wound up even more and launch into another lengthy discourse. Finally, the host minister started responding to every few sentences with 'Amen, Pharaoh!' The guest preacher wasn't sure what that meant, but after several more 'Amen, Pharaohs' he finally concluded his very lengthy sermon. After the service ended and the congregation had left, the visiting minister turned to his host and asked, 'What exactly did you mean when you said "Amen, Pharaoh?" His host replied, 'I was telling you to let my people go!'

Anon.

25 SHOUT IT FROM THE HOUSETOPS

Broadcaster Ali Burnett writes: I grew up in a family which didn't *do* church. But when I did find Christians, I found a whole new world of lively churches, books, holidays, teaching, and fellowship. It took me six years because this 'subculture' wasn't evident on the radio or telly – apart from boring 'churchy' programmes which didn't appeal to me at all. So I deliberately went into media to try and redress the balance. It seemed like the best way of reaching the largest number of non-Christians! Jesus was a broadcaster. He rarely taught one-to-one. His sermons were addressed to large crowds. He used the mass media of His day – a hill, a boat, the Temple courts. He went where people were and fed their hunger to know God.

Once when I'd just come 'off air' after an early Sunday breakfast shift on 31 October, the next presenter opened the microphone following his first record and said 'Ali, you do God. Why don't Christians like Hallowe'en?' I had to stand and deliver in about 30 seconds! What would you have said?! But he really wanted to know. And I was in the place to 'go tell' both him and his largely non-churchgoing audience. Why didn't they know already?

There's a church near me with what I feel is the perfect motto, 'To know Christ, and to make Him known'. Jesus left His church two specific new commandments: one, love each other. Two, go tell. So surely our Christian life should balance that, 50/50. How come it's more 90/10 in favour of the first one? Is it because we're too frightened to deal with the real world? How come every other organisation with a message to put across has a press officer and deals with media ... and yet most churches don't? Media isn't the devil – it just gets used a lot by the devil!

Let's 'go tell' via the media – and be sure of a non-churchgoing audience, instead of hiding away in ghettos where non-Christians are less likely to find us and our Good News.

MAYBE TOMORROW you could pray for Christians who work in the media, that they may be strengthened, protected, and inspired to find ways to 'salt' the programmes people watch and hear and the news they read. And why not encourage your church to appoint a press officer or press team and support their work as a ministry, like any other? Don't be afraid of the media – reclaim it for the Kingdom of God!

Used with permission. Copyright © Ali Burnett 2012 www.churchads.net

NIGHT PRAYER:

Steadfast God, the world is changing at such a pace. At times, today's digital world is confusing and exhausting. Too much information! Yet where is Your Word in the market place of ideas? Equip me and others in the Church to speak for You loudly, clearly and imaginatively, so many will hear. I ask this in the name of Jesus who was the broadcaster of Your Word and also the message itself. Amen.

TM

BIBLE READING:

[Jesus said], 'What I tell you now in the darkness, shout abroad when daybreak comes. What I whisper in your ear, shout from the housetops for all to hear!' **Matthew 10:27, NLT**
Paul in the marketplace **Acts 17:22–32**

FURTHER REFLECTION
BEING CULTURALLY RELEVANT:

God. It's that time of the day again, and I have no idea where the day has gone. Or life, really. Everything seems to rush past so quickly, and often I am struggling to catch my breath. Change is happening all around me in the colours of the trees and car tax discs – even the colour of my hair and the lines now chiselled on my face mean I am sometimes confused by the reflection in the mirror.

In the midst of your technicoloured world, help me to journey through life at the pace your Spirit leads me. Help me to see the glamour of your kingdom rather than the glitz of the promises of chemicals. Give me the appetite to say 'yes' to the things that I dread, and the patience to say 'no' to some of the things that give me comfort. Keep me close to the culture of your Kingdom, and help me to make good and valuable and worthy connections with the cultures in which I live life engaged in – with confidence, clarity and generosity. Amen.

Used with permission. Copyright © Revd Joanne Cox September 2011

@daily_encourage

Fear not, God is awake and works in your favour 24 hours a day!

Hannah Sarah Miles

SMILE:

A stitch in time would have confused Einstein.

Anon.

THE HARDEST WORD

26

How many times have I gone to bed feeling sorry for myself when I should've said 'sorry' to someone else? Too many, I fear. It's human nature to think that the other person is the one who should say 'sorry' first and to be too proud to make the first move. It's times like this I need to remember that *sin* is a three-letter word with 'I' in the middle – it's when the world revolves around me, rather than in service of God and others.

These days, the word 'sorry' seems to trip off the tongue so easily: 'Sorry, could you repeat that?' 'I'm so sorry to hear that.' 'I'm sorry, but that's my decision.' 'I feel so sorry for you.' 'Sorry, this is a long list of quotes.' Polite and often appropriate, but these uses of the word are not nearly as powerful as a real heartfelt apology. That sort of 'sorry' could bring a breakdown in communication to an end. It could also prepare the ground for healing, forgiveness and reconciliation. In these days of instant communication, with so many different ways to do it, there's simply no excuse *not* to say sorry to someone when it's needed and appropriate – whether they are close or many miles away! Why waste time harbouring hurts and being unhappy?

MAYBE TOMORROW you could pluck up courage to utter the 'S' word. Remember: a bend in the road is not the end of the road … unless you fail to make the turn. As for tonight, remember this very practical teaching in the Bible: '"In your anger do not sin": Do not let the sun go down while you are still angry …' (Eph. 4:26). If you don't seek to address your anger or broken relationships at the end of the day, the situation may be worse in the morning. Choose to rise to a day of new beginnings and opportunities.

NIGHT PRAYER:

Gracious God, it's comforting to know that some of the great
characters in the Bible made their mistakes too – even King
David and Peter the Rock. I thank You that You love me
despite my faults and see the potential that is in me. I humbly
bring myself before You with sorrow for my shortcomings and
selfishness; seeking forgiveness for my wrongdoing. Create in
me a clean heart, O God. Renew a right spirit within me, that
I will be prepared to say 'sorry' where necessary, and walk in
the light with my Lord and Saviour Jesus. In His name, I pray.
Amen.[15]

BIBLE READING:

Jesus said, 'For if you forgive men when they sin against you,
your heavenly Father will also forgive you. But if you do not
forgive men their sins, your Father will not forgive your sins.'
Matthew 6:14–15
Do not give the devil a foothold **Ephesians 4:25–5:2**

FURTHER REFLECTION
BEING THANKFUL FOR THE GIFT OF TIME:

Another day, another hour, another minute.

O God, how hard it is for me to get through this time.

Another day, another hour, another minute.

What a gift, gracious God, how shall I fill them?

Help me to see time as a gift from you.

May I look forward to each returning day, full of hope and anticipation.

And when I feel weary, and life is tough, and time drags,

may I remember that each moment is precious;

that once it has gone it cannot be relived.

And at the end of each day, may I rejoice in all it has brought.

Each day, each hour, each moment, lived in your presence.

Amen.

Used with permission. Copyright © Revd Anne Brown February 2009

@daily_encourage

'Is anything too hard for the Lord?' Your current situation certainly isn't! Give it to Him.

Hannah Sarah Miles

SMILE:

'Anger' is just one letter short of 'Danger'.

Anon.

Now there's a new book on the market for people who disagree – a CONTRADICTIONARY.

Anon.

27 NOT QUITE 100%

I admire doctors. Though I've never worked out why they always ask, 'How are you?' when you visit them. It's tempting to reply, 'Sick actually, otherwise I wouldn't be here!' Nevertheless, I respect their experience and the extensive training they've undertaken. GPs have been authorised to practice and have the weight of the NHS behind them. They are mere human beings, but the fact they're qualified makes all the difference: people trust them and benefit from their care.

Jesus came to heal and save a sick world. Matthew 10:1 tells how Jesus '… called his twelve disciples to him and gave them authority to drive out evil spirits and to heal every disease and sickness.' They'd been following and learning from their Teacher's wisdom. Others had tagged along too, but the 'Twelve' were the ones who'd made a wholehearted response. They were to be their Master's special representatives – 'twelve' was reminiscent of the Old Testament tribes of Israel. Jesus said to them, 'The harvest is plentiful but the workers are few. Ask the Lord of the harvest, therefore, to send out workers …' (Matt. 9:37–38). The disciples found themselves landed with the job and, despite their lack of experience and not feeling up to it, the Lord sets about restoring Israel through them – qualifying and authorising them.

How is the world today? Many would reply, 'Sick actually, and in need of help.' Jesus makes His diagnosis and has the cure. Despite my feelings of inadequacy, He is calling ME and YOU to work for Him with the help of the Holy Spirit. Our Lord's friends become wounded healers, used powerfully despite their own vulnerabilities. Remember that when it comes to God's work, it's not *how* you feel or *what* you know, but *who* you know.

MAYBE TOMORROW, even though you may not feel 100%, it's worth remembering that Jesus is your healer. So, may the God of peace '… equip you with everything good for doing his will, and may he work in us what is pleasing to him, through Jesus Christ, to whom be glory for ever and ever. Amen' (Heb. 13:21).

NIGHT PRAYER:

Thank You, Lord, that You are my Healer and answer my prayers according to Your perfect will. Even though I feel totally inadequate at times, I praise You that you don't call the equipped, but equip the called! Amen.

BIBLE READING:

'For I can do everything through Christ, who gives me strength.'
Philippians 4:13, NLT
'To keep me from becoming conceited … there was given me a thorn in my flesh, a messenger of Satan to torment me … [the Lord] said to me "My grace is sufficient for you …"'
2 Corinthians 12:1–10

FURTHER REFLECTION
BEING IN NEED OF HELP:

I call it the HELP prayer.
God my Father, I want to be honest with you; my faith is not great,
but you said it could be small as a grain of mustard seed.
I think, 'Maybe tomorrow I will be healed', but then 'Maybe not'; that's the nagging thought.
So I come to you with my health problem, and I say with the leper who came to Jesus,
'If you are willing, you can make me clean.'
You see God, I know you *can*, but I am not sure you *will* heal.

So, God, this is my specific prayer for help:
Heal me, that is my deepest wish, and grant
Endurance to cope with any treatment I may have, and grant
that I may know I am
Loved by my family and friends, and by you, and grant me your
Peace because I don't want bitterness to enter me, but a trust in you
In Jesus' name, who said: 'I am the resurrection and the life.'
Amen.

Used with permission. Copyright © Revd Dr Malcolm White October 2011

@daily_encourage

Sometimes we have to wait for the promises of God.

Hannah Sarah Miles

SMILE:

Have you a long-standing problem? TRY KNEELING!

Anon.

THE GREAT CLOUD OF WITNESSES 28

When I was a minister in Essex, I used to hold an annual service for those who'd lost loved ones. I would write to those for whom I'd conducted funerals, inviting them to a quiet, informal ceremony. I would read out the names of all who'd died in the last year, together with others who'd died a while ago – whose families were still grieving. The lights were dimmed and we would feel united through our common pain and loss. As beautiful music played, I'd light the first candle to remember the death of Jesus and that He is the Light of the World. Yes, He died. But on the third day He rose again, conquering sin and death. Jesus was and is the Resurrection and the Life, giving hope to all believers. From that first candle, I'd light others in memory of my loved ones. Then, one by one, as people came forward to do the same, the light gradually grew to be a blaze of brightness.

This wasn't a morbid time, but an opportunity to remember loved ones, to shed a tear, pray for one another, and to be reminded of the Christian hope. Life can sometimes feel a hopeless struggle – especially when we are overwhelmed by sorrow or other 'dark nights of the soul'. Yet seeing the mass of candles shining on the table always reminded me of a passage in the Bible where the writer compares the life of faith to a race. All those whose journey of faith has been punctuated by death are now with God because Jesus made life beyond the grave possible. Though they are no longer with us, they are cheering us on from the heavenly places! 'Therefore, since we are surrounded by such a great cloud of witnesses, let us throw off everything that hinders and the sin that so easily entangles. And let us run with perseverance the race marked out for us' (Heb. 12:1). I can imagine my mum, nan, grandad, aunt, uncle, as well as Rob, Chris, John, Norma and a whole host of others, encouraging me to press on, no matter what challenges I face, and to remember the joy that's ultimately set before me.

MAYBE TOMORROW you can remember the great cloud of witnesses who are cheering you on too.

NIGHT PRAYER:

Eternal God, help me to sleep peacefully tonight, that I may run the race tomorrow with my eyes fixed on Jesus. Amen.

BIBLE READING:

Jesus said, 'Peace I leave with you; my peace I give you. I do not give to you as the world gives. Do not let your hearts be troubled and do not be afraid.' **John 14:27**
Running the race **Hebrews 11:32–12:2**

FURTHER REFLECTION
BEING A FRIEND TO SOMEONE WHO IS MOURNING:

I don't know what to say, Lord.
My friend's son has died. It's so tragic.
The family's in shreds and all her friends are distraught.
I want to help, Lord, but I feel so helpless.
I'm out of my depth.
So I'm praying hard, Lord, really hard, for the wisdom of Your Holy Spirit to show me the right words to say.
Her life has crashed around her; please help me to be supportive and sensitive to her needs just now.
Help me to listen and not be embarrassed by tears –
hers or mine.
Lord, open my eyes to practical needs – a lift – a meal – a hug.

Maybe tomorrow You will show me how.
I pray this prayer in and through my Saviour Jesus. Amen.

Used with permission. Copyright © Revd Elizabeth Rundle October 2011

@daily_encourage

God's faithfulness is the same today, tomorrow and forever.
As He has helped others, so He will help you too.

Hannah Sarah Miles

SMILE:

A little girl was being shown around a big cathedral. She stared in awe at a great stained glass window. The summer sun streamed through, bathing the cathedral floor in colour. She asked the tour guide, 'Who are those people in the pretty window?' 'Those are the saints,' he said. Later, at bedtime, the girl told her mother, 'I know who the saints are.' 'Do you, dear,' said Mum, 'who are they then?' 'They're the people who let the light shine through.'

Anon.

BEING EFFECTIVE

Almighty God, we are so good at talking.
We excel at holding meetings and taking minutes.
Forgive our tendency for endless words.

By the power of Your Holy Spirit,
turn our words into actions,
serving others as You also served.

Forgive us when we sit back in the armchairs of our
comfortable world,
watching others in crisis and pain.

Lord, help us to engage our faith,
to be involved,
not standing at a distance,
but in participation with our neighbours,
that we may truly be Your Church,
kneeling before our communities with humility and
compassion:
supporting the vulnerable,
seeking the lost,
searching out the lonely,
welcoming the stranger,
with Your transforming love. Amen.

Used with permission. Copyright © Deacon Eunice Atwood January 2010

THE WAY AND WORDS

Now don't you let the troubles of tomorrow
Bring sadness to your heart and burdens too;
For if the Father's eye is on the sparrow
Then surely He will care for you.
He knoweth, He careth, each burden He beareth,
For if the Father's eye is on the sparrow
Then surely He will care for you.

Anon.

29 STRANGERS

Are you just a bit strange? I ask because I wish I were more of a 'stranger' in the world. By that I don't mean weird, remote or disinterested. After all, Jesus befriended people and didn't hide Himself away. No, I'm talking about the need for Christians to be strangers to the ways of the world because they are different! In that sense, it's good for me to be 'slightly strange', for it means I'm counter-cultural in a predominantly secular society. It's biblical, too! 1 Peter 1:1 says, 'Peter, an apostle of Jesus Christ, To God's elect, *strangers* in the world ...' Then later in verse 17: 'Since you call on a Father who judges each man's work impartially, live your lives as strangers here in reverent fear.' What's more, Peter says God's obedient children are 'to be holy in all [we] do'. That doesn't mean I'm to be 'holier-than-thou' and a bit odd. Rather, it's being holy in the sense that my Maker is transforming me and setting me apart. So, when God says 'Be holy, because I am holy', it involves my becoming a stranger to the habits of an ungodly world. With the help of the Holy Spirit, I'm to grow in holiness by bearing the fruit of a right and deepening relationship with my heavenly Father through Jesus. I'm to let Him be the 'friendly driving instructor' in my life, inspiring me to travel the right way – which will often be against the flow.

MAYBE TOMORROW people will think you're 'slightly strange'. So be it. The important thing is that you'll not be a 'stranger' to God if you live for Him. Surely that's what matters more than anything else.

NIGHT PRAYER:

Lord, others may snigger because I'm living for You, but tomorrow may I picture Jesus' approving gaze and return a knowing smile in Your direction. Amen.

BIBLE READING:

'I am the LORD, who brought you up out of Egypt to be your God; therefore be holy, because I am holy.' **Leviticus 11:45**
Strangers in the world' **1 Peter 1:1–25**

FURTHER REFLECTION
BEING A WORLD-CHANGING DISCIPLE:

God whose love disturbs and challenges
   Transform us, we pray

God whose love is lavish and everlasting
   Transform us, we pray

God whose love revives and renews
   Transform us, we pray

God whose love is unbounding and unchanging
   Transform us we pray

By our words and our actions
Enable us to engage our faith
Equip us to be Your people
Courageous, risk-takers
Transformed by the Spirit of God
Confident in the love of God
Life-affirming, world-changing
Disciples of Christ. Amen.

Used with permission. Copyright © Deacon Eunice Atwood January 2010

@daily_encouragee

The Lord is at work in you and He will finish what He has begun!

Hannah Sarah Miles

SMILE:

It's all right for a perfect stranger to kiss your hand as long as he's perfect.

Mae West – American actress and playwright (1893–1980)

SAFARI

Mike Giles writes: Several years ago I felt that the phrase 'Journey of Faith or Life' had become overused; it had lost its power to challenge. 'Journey' also suggested a straight path or road from A to B. Then I came across the Swahili word for journey, which is 'safari'. Now that sounds much more interesting, and it brings alive a new way of thinking about faith. You choose which safari to go on and there is usually an expert driver and guide. There will be fellow travellers, surprises, new sights and experiences, some exhilarating, others scary. The important thing, if you want to get to the end safely, is to listen to the guide and trust the driver to negotiate the rough terrain.

MAYBE TOMORROW you can apply those thoughts to your faith so it becomes alive. God is the Driver of our life, the Holy Spirit the Guide and Jesus is our Fellow Traveller. The Bible is full of individuals, families and people on the move. Abraham left his home on a new journey of discovery, Moses wandered for forty years in the desert, Mary and Joseph made the dangerous safari to Bethlehem, Jesus took twelve fellow-travellers on his safaris, and Paul had his amazing missionary journeys. The Church is a movement!

NIGHT PRAYER:

God of Safari, in the marketplace of religious tourist brochures, may we choose a safari with Jesus as Friend and Companion, Help us to listen to the whispers of the expert guiding Spirit, to follow You more closely through the bush and rough roads of life.
Thank You for new friendships, cultures, music and insights. Feed us with enough spiritual food to satisfy and spice up our souls,

and may we find in the desert of life Jesus the oasis of pure
living water.

Keep us safe as we white water raft through the canyons of life's
turbulent waters,

trusting that You will take us to safety of dry land.

May we be open to new experiences, learning from and sharing
them with others.

Holy Spirit, enable us to see beyond the end of a photo lens,

to hear different sounds and to keep alert our spiritual senses.

We ask for a good night's sleep as we camp through life,

that we find rest and renewal to face the next day.

The end of this safari may be in sight, but with You there are
always new adventures.

Excite us about Safari of Life and Faith.

In the name of God our Driver, Jesus our Fellow Traveller,
and Holy Spirit our Guide. Amen.

Used with permission. Copyright © Revd Michael G Giles March 2011

BIBLE READING:

'Jesus said to Simon, "There is nothing to fear. From now on
you'll be fishing for men and women." They pulled their boats
up on the beach, left them, nets and all, and followed him.'
Luke 5:10–11, *The Message*
Abraham leaves home **Genesis 12:1–20**

FURTHER REFLECTION
BEING A TRUSTING TRAVELLER:

Brought safely by His hand thus far,
Why wilt thou now give place to fear?
How canst thou want if He provide,
Or lose thy way with such a guide?

*John Newton – British sailor and Anglican clergyman
(1725–1807)*

@daily_encourage

There is no map like the Word; there is no satnav like the Spirit; there is no journey-planner like God.

Hannah Sarah Miles

SMILE:

When you have completed 95% of your journey, you are only halfway there.

Japanese proverb

31 A SONG TO SING?

I love to sing. Others might not appreciate my singing, but that doesn't bother me in the slightest – especially in the shower! My voice isn't bad, despite a lack of musical training – just loud. Thankfully, when I worship alone or in church, I believe God is more interested in whether I have a song to sing, than my qualifications.

I'm reminded of the words of King David: 'I will praise you, O Lord, among the nations; I will sing of you among the peoples. For great is your love, reaching to the heavens; your faithfulness reaches to the skies. Be exalted, O God, above the heavens; let your glory be over all the earth' (Psa. 57:9–11). At one time, David had been crouching in the dark corner of a cave whilst being pursued by the jealous King Saul. But there's a contrast in this psalm. David is now standing tall in confidence and faith. Most people would've been content with withdrawing from the enemy and finding refuge in God. But, despite the challenges he faced, David perseveres, looks heavenwards, and finds new vision and strength. This overflows in a song of praise giving testimony to God's loving nature and truth. He worships the Lord who has faithfully kept His promises, declaring that praise shall fill the universe, together with God's mercy and truth.

MAYBE TOMORROW when the pressure is on, you can find sanctuary in God too. Draw strength from praise and devotion. Worship leader, Matt Redman, wrote these lyrics: 'If you know you're loved by the King, then sing, sing, sing …'[16]

NIGHT PRAYER:

'You awaken us to delight in your praise; for you have made us for yourself, and our hearts are restless until they find their rest in you.' Amen.

St Augustine of Hippo – influential Christian thinker, philosopher/theologian (354–430)

BIBLE READING:

'Speak to one another with psalms, hymns and spiritual songs. Sing and make music in your heart to the Lord, always giving thanks to God the Father for everything, in the name of our Lord Jesus Christ.' **Ephesians 5:19–20**
A Psalm for Giving Thanks **Psalm 100**

FURTHER REFLECTION
BEING 'IN ADORATION':

In adoration I come before You
To bow in reverent awe with gratitude and love
For You have won my heart
My grand illusions of self-importance
Are melted like the snow when spring starts drawing near
Lord, You have won my heart

For there is no-one like You;
Yes, there is no-one like You.
I've seen what You can do and I want to tell You now
That You have won my heart

Used with permission. Copyright © 2011 Dave Bilbrough Songs www.davebilbrough.com Taken from the album Precious Grace

@daily_encourage

Praise Him for Who He is: the Lord of Lords and King of Kings! Worship not only brings Him joy ... but us too!

Hannah Sarah Miles

SMILE:

Why was the lead singer standing outside the church? He didn't have the 'key' and didn't know when to 'come in'.

Anon.

MAY THE WORDS OF MY MOUTH

32

There's an old Jewish proverb, 'Nothing causes more trouble than the tongue'. Can you think of times today when you've said something you've really regretted? Words used carelessly and without restraint can be incredibly destructive. Insults, lies, gossip, bragging and blasphemy can change the direction of our lives, and others; they can lead people into trouble and away from God. Benjamin Franklin said, 'A slip of the foot you may soon recover, but a slip of the tongue you may never get over.' So ask God to forgive you and learn from your mistakes.

In the New Testament, James compares the tongue's power to the bit in a horse's mouth that can change the animal's direction, and to the rudder on a ship that can change its course. The tongue may only be small, but it is very influential and its boasts reveal what our hearts are really like. So, the tongue is difficult to control and yet powerful enough to control the whole body. If we gain control of our tongues, we gain control of other areas of our lives too. Just as a horse's bit needs a rider to pull the reins, and a rudder needs a pilot to steer, so the tongue needs the Holy Spirit's guidance. Harnessed effectively, our words can then lead us away from sin – especially if we use them to ask for forgiveness, or to praise or bless God and other people.

MAYBE TOMORROW you could pay attention to what comes out of your mouth and use words carefully and creatively. Remember also to name the name of Jesus – the true Word of God. Unless you speak of Him, others may never get to know Him.

NIGHT PRAYER:

Father, forgive the trouble I have caused with my tongue. Help me never to underestimate its power, but train it to boast of You alone; to bless and not to curse, and to speak truth rather than lies. In Jesus' name. Amen.

BIBLE READING:

Jesus said, 'For out of the overflow of the heart the mouth speaks.' **Matthew 12:34**
Taming the Tongue **James 3:1–12**

FURTHER REFLECTION
BEING NOT GRUMPY:

Why is it, Lord, that people being grumpy on the
TV is 'entertainment'?
Suddenly, I find myself becoming grumpy too,
but in the 'real' world, my day-to-day routines,
people who are grumpy are not entertaining!
Lord, I pray forgiveness for the times
when I've *enjoyed* being grumpy, and for times
when my grumps have hindered the Gospel.
Forgive me, too, when my grumps have been
sour and hurtful for those around me.
Forgive me and restore a better attitude in my
heart. In the power of Your Spirit, maybe
tomorrow I will remember to think before I
speak. Thank You, Lord, that tomorrow is a
fresh start, a new day to live in Your Light
and Life and Joy. Amen.

Used with permission. Copyright © Revd Elizabeth Rundle September 2011

@daily_encourage

Let's encourage each other through our words tomorrow and say only what helps. Treat each word as a gift to another person.

Hannah Sarah Miles

SMILE?

The best way to save face is to keep the lower part of it shut.

Anon.

33 WIN SOME, LOSE SOME

I lost a couple of stone by following a special diet. I think I should be put on commission: so many people are now giving the method a try, thinking, 'If Tony can do it, then so can I.' I feel better for it and it's been part of my getting into rhythm (as mentioned earlier in this book). Some say dieting is a matter of the will, but someone more accurately said it's more about 'won't'!

I don't mention all this to encourage dieting, but to point out that some – who rather insensitively told me I 'needed to lose weight' – are now the ones asking, 'Are you ill? You are looking too thin, you know.' I can't win. It's a good job I didn't shed the pounds for them! What's more, it's often the same folk who point out that I'm losing my hair – as if it had somehow escaped my attention. I've been so tempted to comment on their personal appearance in return, but thought better of it.

We have to be careful about the comments we make about each other. Being in the public eye, I try not to be an overly delicate flower, but we're all sensitive underneath our bravado. It's no wonder that some people end up with eating disorders, or become depressed or insecure. I'm the first to have a joke and to tease my friends, but I need to really know those I'm having fun with and be sure they know when I'm being serious or not. I also need to know the fine line between harmless banter and insensitive, cheap or hurtful jibes. Keeping healthy is important, but we can also get screwed up about appearances, when God wants us to be happy in our own skin and secure in His love.

MAYBE TOMORROW you can remember that your weight, physique, complexion, hairstyle or amount of friends you have aren't the most important things. Not compared to your relationship with God through Christ, and the light that shines out through you. Why not gently challenge ugly criticisms this week?

NIGHT PRAYER:

Merciful Lord, forgive me for not being careful with my tongue today. When necessary, rein in my humour and any spite in the day ahead. Help me to pay meaningful compliments – especially affirming inner beauty, in Your name. Amen.

BIBLE READING:

'Pleasant words are a honeycomb, sweet to the soul and healing to the bones.' **Proverbs 16:24**
Listening and Doing **James 1:19–27**

FURTHER REFLECTION
BEING AWARE OF SENSES:

Holy God, using all my senses of sight, sound and touch,
Through what I say, may I proclaim the Gospel of Christ Jesus
Through those I touch, may I bring Your healing and comfort
To those I meet, a sense of Your joy and peace
Through the firmness of my faith, hope to those who
are searching
Through the genuineness of my love,
a glimpse of the love You have for all Your creation. Amen.

Used with permission. Copyright © Deacon Denise Creed August 2011

@daily_encourage

See yourself as God sees you. Not how the world sees you.

Hannah Sarah Miles

SMILE:

People who are forced to eat their own words should find it a good diet to reduce their big mouths.

Anon.

A real friend will tell you if you have spinach stuck on your teeth.

Anon.

GIVING A REASON 34

Justin Brierley writes: I've often said, 'I don't have enough faith to be an atheist.' There's too much order, too much meaning, too much love and too much beauty for this world to be the chance accident of a godless universe. But then my sceptical friends tell me there's too much pain, too much disorder, and too many questions left unanswered for this world to be the result of a God-filled universe.

The questions of my friends will always remain tough and how we answer them may vary, but the way we do it should not.

MAYBE TOMORROW you could offer an answer to the person who asks you that difficult question. Not putting up barriers of defence, but starting a conversation with gentleness, grace and respect.

NIGHT PRAYER:

God of All – with gentleness and respect:
Give me ears to listen to others' questions and treat them seriously.
With gentleness and respect:
Form in me a mind to understand the reason for the hope I have within.
With gentleness and respect:
Grant to me the speech that says with confidence where I stand and why.
In hearing, understanding and speaking
may I share Your love with all my strength, with all my soul and with all my mind.
In Jesus' name. Amen.

BIBLE READING:

'But in your hearts set apart Christ as Lord. Always be prepared to give an answer to everyone who asks you to give the reason for the hope that you have. But do this with gentleness and respect ...' **1 Peter 3:15**

Keep Your Head **2 Timothy 3:14–4:8**

FURTHER REFLECTION
BEING HONEST:

Loving God, am I alone in finding my life very complicated?
As a Christian I try hard to follow in Your way,
but the decisions I have to make often seem so complex and the way ahead not at all clear.
All I can offer You is my best!
I bring that to You now and pray that You will take my offer,
by Your Holy Spirit help me to pick my way through the complications
and then make real Your Word that all things work together for the good of those who love You.
Lord I do love You.
I offer you my best.
Help me to leave the rest to You. Amen.

Used with permission. Copyright © Revd Martin Turner September 2011
www.methodist-central-hall.org.uk

@daily_encourage

You don't need to hold or cling on to God, because He's already holding on to you!

Hannah Sarah Miles

Atheism is a non-prophet organisation.

Anon.

35 THE LIVING WORD

Canon Michael Cole writes: Five teenagers sat around Joe's kitchen table, I was one of them. I didn't want to miss our weekly meeting reading God's *Living* Word. That was years ago, yet God's Word is still *active* in my life, showing me what is right and what is wrong.

Teenagers – and that includes our grandchildren – still sit round the table. It's Facebook or Twitter they're reading. They are growing up in a world that doesn't know the Lord's Prayer, the Ten Commandments, The Sermon on the Mount, nor the love, power and grace of God, Father, Son and Holy Spirit.

MAYBE TOMORROW more people will turn to God's Living Word on the website or their iPad, or treasure their own Bible as much as they treasure their Man United football shirt. Maybe tomorrow we shall come back to being an openly confessing Christian community, loving and caring for the world in which we live and seeking to please, not ourselves, but the Lord who loves us and gave Himself for us.

NIGHT PRAYER:

Lord, how can a young man keep his way pure? By living according to Your Word. Help me to *seek* You with all my heart, don't let me stray from your commands. I have *hidden* Your word in my heart. I don't want to sin against You. Lord, may that be true for teenagers facing tomorrow.

Used with permission. Copyright © Canon Michael Cole September 2011
www.nationwidechristiantrust.com

BIBLE READING:

'For the word of God is living and active. Sharper than any double-edged sword, it penetrates even to dividing soul and spirit, joints and marrow; it judges the thoughts and attitudes of the heart.' **Hebrews 4:12**

Living according to the Word **Psalm 119:9–11**

FURTHER REFLECTION
BEING RECEPTIVE:

In the rush and noise of life,
help us wait upon you, O Lord.
Within ourselves may we be still and know you to be our God.
Day by day let us rejoice in the light of your presence;
through Jesus Christ our Lord. Amen.

William Penn – English Quaker and the founder of the colony of Pennsylvania (1644–1718)

@daily_encourage

The better we know the Bible, the better we can know the will and nature of God!

Hannah Sarah Miles

SMILE:

Who was the greatest financier in the Bible?
Noah. *He was floating his stock while everyone else was in liquidation.*

Who was the greatest female financier in the Bible?
Pharaoh's daughter. She went down to the bank of the Nile and drew out a little prophet.

Anon.

BEING IN AWE OF THE CREATOR
IN THE BEGINNING

Genesis 1. Musings on a Quiet Day:

DAY 1: Light came through the stained glass window in the church, the same light that God spoke into being on that first day long, long ago. Colours in the glass were brought to life by that same ancient light – beautiful, swirling – red, orange, blue green, brown, grey, lilac, turquoise – what a delight!

And what will tomorrow bring?

DAY 2: From high on the cliff top my eyes were drawn to the far horizon, the dividing line between the sea and the sky. A cargo ship, so small, crawled along that line to an unknown destination. Is it possible that God knew on His second creative day that I would be here and the ship would be there?

I don't know – perhaps tomorrow I will.

DAY 3: The apples were red and tempting as we walked the path on the hill, enjoying the beauty of the landscape around us. We all picked one and our teeth sank into the crunchy, juicy, Oh so tasty fruit – heaven! Thank You God for the bounty of the third day.

What will You do tomorrow?

DAY 4: The desert sun was hot – it's like that in an Arizona summer – but I was grateful, for the sun made it possible for me to see the way ahead and my sure-footed horse knew the way better than I. I went out that night and looked up at the sky – and I gasped at the beauty of the stars – so many, so big and seeming so near that I thought I could touch them, pick one and take it home. My heart wanted to burst with the glory of it! I'm excited at the thought of tomorrow, Lord!

DAY 5: I'll never forget the dolphin in the pool – as I looked

through the glass, it glided by, glanced at me and tipped its head – such a little thing but I felt privileged. So too on the day I saw a flight of black kites, rare creatures now – swirling and swooping overhead. I wish I could fly with them!
You never know, maybe tomorrow it will be so.

DAY 6: So Lord, You left the cows and the cats and the creepy-crawlies until today – what a treat! How empty life would be without them. But what is more amazing is that the icing on the cake is us – and in Your image and likeness too.
What actually does that mean Lord?

We cannot do what You have done but what we can do, we can do with generosity like Yours. We cannot speak as You did and form stars and songbirds, but what we do say can be life giving, not destructive. We can bless as You did and not curse. We can recognise what is good as You did and not spoil what is beautiful.
It's been a full six days Lord and I'm tired. I need a rest.
See You tomorrow Lord.

DAY 7: You've thought of everything haven't You? You knew I needed a break – and here I am having one! Oh, the luxury of just enjoying the day with You. After all You've done for me it's the least I can do – and actually this day is a very precious gift.
Is there something I can do for You Lord?

And God said: 'Maybe tomorrow.'

Used with permission. Copyright © Christine Watts September 2011

THROUGH THE YEAR 1

Sometimes a light surprises
The Christian while he sings;
It is the Lord who rises
With healing in his wings:
When comforts are declining,
He grants the soul again
A season of clear shining,
To cheer it after rain.

In holy contemplation,
We sweetly then pursue
The theme of God's salvation,
And find it ever new.
Set free from present sorrow,
We cheerfully can say,
Now let the unknown morrow
Bring with it what it may:

It can bring with it nothing
But he will bear us through;
Who gives the lilies clothing
Will clothe his people too:
Beneath the spreading heavens
No creature but is fed;
And he who feeds the ravens
Will give his children bread.

Though vine nor fig-tree neither
Their wonted fruit should bear,
Though all the field should wither,
Nor flocks nor herds be there,
Yet, God the same abiding,
His praise shall tune my voice;
For, while in him confiding,
I cannot but rejoice.

*William Cowper – English hymn writer
and poet (1731–1800)*

HOW TO PACK A PUNCH (CHRISTIAN UNITY)

36

If the Christian Church is a family, then we shouldn't be surprised if we don't always agree with each other or share the same tastes – despite being in the same 'life-bloodline'. I love the work of cartoonist Charles Schulz (1922–2000) and was pleased to discover www.peanuts.com. One comic strip is often quoted when we think about the Church and unity. It was when Lucy van Pelt demanded that her little brother, Linus, changed the TV channel. She threatened him with her fist if he didn't do it. Linus asks why she thinks she can just come in and assume control. Lucy shows him her fingers and says separately they are nothing, but once curled together into one they make a frightening weapon. Linus immediately lets her choose the channel, and walks away, staring at his hand, asking his fingers why they can't get co-ordinated like that.

MAYBE TOMORROW you can 'get organised' with your fellow Christians by getting on with the work Jesus gave us to do. Watch out! It's easy to throw unnecessary 'religious punches' in the form of condescending jibes at those whose thinking or behaviour is different from yours. Be generous.

NIGHT PRAYER:

Three-in-One God, thank You for the richness of Christian diversity. May I respect difference and not be frightened of it. Help me to find unity in love and purpose with my sisters and brothers in Christ. Amen.

BIBLE READING:

'How good and pleasant it is when brothers live together in unity!
It is like precious oil poured on the head, running down on
the beard, running down on Aaron's beard, down upon the
collar of his robes. It is as if the dew of Hermon were falling on
Mount Zion. For there the LORD bestows his blessing, even life
for evermore.' **Psalm 133**
Jesus prays for His disciples and all believers **John 17**

FURTHER REFLECTION
BEING UNITED:

Almighty Creator, You alone are our God – worthy of all our
praise and worship.
You gave us the gift of life and made us to live in community.
You want us to celebrate our diversity, but to discover that You
are a God of unity
who longs for us to be one just as You are one, so that the world
may believe.
With many tongues and yet with one voice, we worship
You together.
We adore You for all that You are and for the hope that You
give to our broken and fragile world.
We praise You that You have not abandoned us, but desire
us to turn towards Your love, and seek Your healing and
reconciliation in all our relationships.
You have sent Your Holy Spirit to work in our hearts, to draw
us closer to You and to one another.
We confess with shame our stubbornness, independence and
selfishness; our intolerance, our pride, and our insensitivity
towards others.
We freely admit our lack of desire to live in harmony with You
and with one another.
Forgive us we pray, and may we be assured of Your pardon,
through our Saviour, Jesus.
May Your grace and mercy permeate our very being; may we be

truly cleansed, renewed, and remade into our Lord's likeness.
For we ask this prayer in His name, that we may be
living stones,
building upon the Rock for the sake of Your kingdom. Amen.

TM

@daily_encourage

When the world is screaming, 'Just give up.' God whispers,
'Just keep going, your breakthrough is soon.'

Hannah Sarah Miles

SMILE:

Jim Wilson, church chairman, urged the congregation to put
principles aside and do what was right.

Anon. – Blooper

37 MOTHER OF A THOUSAND BLESSINGS (MOTHERING SUNDAY)

A 102-year-old lady was asked if she had any worries. 'No,' she replied, 'Not now I've got my youngest son into an old people's home!' I guess parents never stop worrying about their children. If you're a mum or a dad, you'll know exactly what I mean. If not, just think of the times you must have caused parents or guardians to worry about you. Never give up praying for your children or other youngsters you can help and influence. What's more, don't forget to keep praying for parents, especially as the tables are turned and you become responsible for a parent who needs support and care. Remember that prayer changes things and God's answers are wiser than our prayers.

Today isn't always an easy day, especially for those of us who are remembering mothers who've died. Nevertheless, we can still celebrate, and be thankful for good, wholesome parenting that we've known, or seen about us. We can also reflect on our own response to the fifth commandment: 'honour your father and your mother' (Exod. 20:12).

Mothering Sunday has also traditionally been a time for Christians to give thanks for the care of 'Mother Church' and think about God's love for us too. Why not pray for the pastoral care of the Church this evening? It's easy to blame others for the Church's failures, but as somebody once said, 'If the church wants a better pastor, it only needs to pray for the one it has.' Similarly, if we want a more caring and nurturing church, we need to pray for each other: for we *are* the Church!

MAYBE TOMORROW you could think about these words of the Archbishop of Constantinople, Saint John of Chrysostom (347–407): 'Prayer is an all-efficient panoply, a treasure undiminished, a mine which is never exhausted, a sky unobscured by clouds, a heaven unruffled by the storm. It is the root, the fountain, the mother of a thousand blessings.'

NIGHT PRAYER:

Caring God, tonight we praise You for mothers past and present. None would claim to be perfect, but we give thanks for their unconditional love and tender hearts; for their concern for our welfare; for their patience and devotion; for their healing and strength, for their energy and skills; for their influence upon our lives; for their hopes and dreams.
On this Mothering Sunday, embrace them in Your arms.
Renew, refresh and bless them.
For in all good mothers and fathers, we catch a glimpse of Your perfect love for us. Amen.

BIBLE READING:

Jesus said, 'O Jerusalem, Jerusalem, you who kill the prophets and stone those sent to you, how often I have longed to gather your children together, as a hen gathers her chicks under her wings, but you were not willing!' **Luke 13:34**
The boy Jesus at the Temple **Luke 2:41–52**

FURTHER REFLECTION
BEING FAMILY:

'A father to the fatherless, a defender of widows, is God in his holy dwelling. God sets the lonely in families ...' says Psalm 68:5–6. Sometimes we especially need to be cared for and, if we don't have a family of our own nearby, what a comfort to be adopted into someone else's. I can think of various occasions when Christian sisters and brothers loved and were 'family' to me. Jesus taught the astonishing truth that God is our loving heavenly Father. When He explained this to His disciples Jesus used the Aramaic word 'Abba' which means 'Daddy'. So, the Creator of the universe with infinite power and knowledge; the Holy God of all purity who will one day judge this world; the One we cannot see but find through faith (that 'decision to trust') – He's Father of the biggest family there ever was or will be. And we can belong to it!

Used with permission. Copyright © Celia Bowring October 2011 www.care.org.uk

@daily_encourage

Esther is an amazing example of God using ordinary people to do AMAZING things. He'll use you if you're willing ... for such a time as this!

Hannah Sarah Miles

SMILE:

One summer evening during a violent thunderstorm a mother was tucking her small boy into bed. She was about to turn off the light when he asked with a tremor in his voice, 'Mummy, will you sleep in my bedroom tonight?' His mother smiled and gave him a reassuring hug. 'I can't dear,' she said. 'I have to sleep in Daddy's room.' A long silence was broken at last by his little voice. 'The big sissy.'

Anon.

'VIVA FOREVER'? (THE TRANSFIGURATION)

38

Several years ago I accompanied my teenage daughter, Hannah, for an exhilarating experience. From a high place, her spirit was lifted. A long awaited reunion had arrived. Her hopes were confirmed. She was spellbound with wonder as she caught a vision of light and an awesome spectacle before her. Thousands shared this encounter too. From a lofty place Hannah saw …
a Spice Girls concert at the O2 Arena!

Now, whatever you think of the Spice Girls, this minister thoroughly enjoyed escorting his daughter. From the age of six, Hannah had been an avid fan. It was wonderful seeing the delight on her face that evening. She was so captivated, so enthralled, that she didn't want to return home. Eventually I coaxed her away. She was beaming, singing and wanting to tell everyone about it. I'm sure you've had similar times, like special acts of worship, which you wanted to last forever because they might never come again in quite the same way.

The Transfiguration happened when three disciples saw Jesus on a mountain. His appearance changed and His clothes shone. The prophets Moses and Elijah appeared by Him. Then we read, 'As the men were leaving Jesus, Peter said to him, "Master, it is good for us to be here"' (Luke 9:33). Peter wanted to capture this breath-taking moment forever: to build shelters for these three important guys in the hope they would stick around. He wanted to enshrine this fleeting vision – just as Moses did with the Tent of Meeting (Exod. 33). Peter was sincere, but wrong. Jesus couldn't stay on the mountain. He had to make His way down to Jerusalem. In fact, the true 'glory' of that moment could only be understood in the light of His looming death on a cross. Our journey through life sometimes rises to the peaks, but often we must travel along the routine of the plains, and even follow the road that drops to the valley depths. We can't stay on a 'high' all the time, but must descend to face everyday challenges if we're to fulfil our calling.

MAYBE TOMORROW you will need to let Jesus go with you through the difficult places or the routine. Often it's there that His love and glory can shine brightly, and lives can be significantly transformed.

NIGHT PRAYER:

Wherever the road takes me tomorrow, Lord, may my special encounters with You sustain me, and remind me of Your faithful promises. Amen.

BIBLE READING:

Jesus said, 'I have brought you glory on earth by completing the work you gave me to do.' **John 17:4**
The Transfiguration **Luke 9:28–36**

FURTHER REFLECTION
BEING SET IN A 'FRAGILE CASE':

Your glory, seen in a life of grace.
Your glory, set in a fragile case.
Lord take my brokenness; the pain, the fears, lost dreams.
Surrendered now to you, dependent on your grace.
For who am I without you?
Lost without hope.
But now that I've found you; I have a new home.
You my creator, shaping this heart.

Come craft in me your plans.
Hold me.
Christ in me, Christ in me, Christ in me:
Your glory, God's mystery. (Repeat)

Used with permission. Words and Music Copyright © Jonathan Green 2010
www.safehousesounds.co.uk

@daily_encourage

You are in the protecting arms of a loving God. You are part of
His plan and He will lead you to great things.

Hannah Sarah Miles

SMILE:
Why shouldn't Christians watch TV? At the transfiguration,
Jesus said, 'Tell the vision to no one.'

Anon.

39 DUST TO DUST (ASH WEDNESDAY)

'Pancake Day' (Shrove Tuesday) is still a popular tradition in many households. Loads of delicious pancakes with lashings of toppings; my favourite being maple syrup – scrummy. I usually ensure I do the cooking, because I enjoy the challenge and pressure of mass production. Nothing to do with being able to pick the best pancakes for yourself, of course. I also like to hone my skill at pancake tossing, hopefully without dropping the best ones on the kitchen floor. The Christian tradition of using up cooking ingredients before Lent is long-standing. Though I doubt many actually prepared to pray and fast!

Today is Ash Wednesday – which has absolutely nothing to do with any burnt pancakes and more to do with dirty faces. Many churches still mark the occasion literally by putting the sign of the cross on people's foreheads. They use ash from last year's burnt palm crosses and say the words, 'for dust you are and to dust you will return' (Gen. 3:19). It's a day for sober reflection as we remember that one day our lives (as we know them) will end. No one has to ask, 'Is there death after life?' but rather, 'Is there life after death?' People don't know when they will die, but when the time comes for me, will I be ready to meet my Maker? Would I be happy with what people say about me at my funeral if I were to die today? Am I ready to give an account of my life to God? This kind of reflection should send me to my knees to seek God's forgiveness and mourn my faithlessness and ungodliness. Wearing ashes may be helpful for some, but what's more important is honest private reflection before a Holy God; prayer that leads to a changed heart and a life lived for King Jesus.

MAYBE TOMORROW you could resolve to turn away
from wrongdoing and look God's holiness and love in the face.
Then trust His mercy, receive forgiveness, and seek to live the
Christian life more urgently in the power of the Spirit.

NIGHT PRAYER:

God of judgment and mercy, forgive me in Jesus' name, and
help me to forgive others. Cleanse me from my sin, create a new
and right spirit within me, and keep me in life eternal. Amen.

BIBLE READING:

'For as in Adam all die, so in Christ all will be made alive.'
1 Corinthians 15:22
Create in me a clean heart **Psalm 51**

FURTHER REFLECTION
BEING FORGIVING:

Lord, thank You for Your incredible demonstrations
of forgiveness.
Thank You that, in times when I can't forgive others
immediately, You accept my 'commitment to forgive'.
During this season of Lent help me continue on my journey
of forgiveness,
daily remembering Your example, Your teaching and Your
Spirit who empowers me.
Nudge me out of any thought patterns which hold me back,
keeping my mind and heart in prison.
Give me resolve to continue speaking out my forgiveness when
I'm at risk of going back over old ground.
Turn my eyes to the future, to the hope You bring, to the
impossible made possible by You.
And when I'm standing strong, looking to the future, with a
lightness in my step, my burden lifted, my heart free, remind

me again what it cost You to forgive me.

May my forgiveness reflect Your forgiveness, my grace reflect Your grace, my love reflect Your love.

For Your glory, Amen.

Used with permission. Copyright © Felicity Green November 2011

@daily_encourage

Whatever situation you may be in today, change is possible.
It's possible through Him. For nothing is impossible for Jesus.

Hannah Sarah Miles

SMILE:

God has promised forgiveness to your repentance, but He has not promised tomorrow to your procrastination.

St Augustine of Hippo – influential Christian thinker, philosopher/theologian (354–430)

ARE YOU BEING SERVED? (MAUNDY THURSDAY)

40

I'd wondered about asking the congregation to wash each other's feet, but thought better of it. Instead, I asked them to let me wash their hands. It was a Maundy Thursday service when we were remembering that Jesus showed the extent of His love by washing His disciples' feet the night before He died. I could tell that some people were still cautious about having their hands washed, let alone feet! But I reminded them how Jesus told Peter that if he objected to being washed, then he couldn't be part of what Christ was doing. Needless to say, everyone came forward as music from Taizé was played. It was extremely moving.

As I gently washed people's hands, it was fascinating seeing how individual everyone's hands were and how differently each person reacted. My back was aching terribly by the end of the service: to do the job properly I had to lean at a difficult angle, but determined to keep going after all Christ had done for me. Afterwards, some told me that they hadn't had their hands washed since they were children, or since they were last in hospital. I tried to do a good job, but some people couldn't resist helping – especially when it came to the drying – when they thought I hadn't done a good job and there were still areas that needed drying more effectively. I wondered what the disciples felt when Jesus washed their feet. Did they dare help, or comment?

'Maundy' comes from the Latin *Mandatum novum do vobis*: 'A new command I give you: ...' (John 13:34). Jesus' last mandate was 'Love one another. As I have loved you, so you must love one another.' Remember what Jesus told His disciples,

'So if I, the Master and Teacher, washed your feet, you must now wash each other's feet. I've laid down a pattern for you. What I've done, you do' (John 13:14–15, *The Message*). We are to give ourselves in service to others, and when the time is right, we must humbly let others serve us.

MAYBE TOMORROW you could look for opportunities to serve others gently and with great love; or it may be that you could encourage or pray for others who serve; or that you need to let others serve you – even if you think you could do a better job!

NIGHT PRAYER:

Thank You, Lord, for opportunities to serve You today. I am sorry for those times when I've been too proud to let others help me. Bless all who will serve others in their daily work tomorrow, doing jobs that I could never do. May they be sustained in all they do and find the encouragement they need to serve well. Amen.

BIBLE READING:

"'No," said Peter, "you shall never wash my feet." Jesus answered, "Unless I wash you, you have no part with me."'
John 13:8
The Last Mandate **John 13:1–38**

FURTHER REFLECTION
BEING PRAYERFUL FOR CARERS IN RESIDENTIAL HOMES:

Thank you, Father God, for men and women who work in
care homes
caring for those nearing the end of their lives;
Thank you for their work, their patience, and their kindness.
Help them Lord to have energy and humour,
And reveal to them, by your Spirit, that we are all eternal beings,
Pilgrims just passing through,
That they might honour the 'thou' in each one,
and if they don't already know You, begin to find the Way,
themselves. Amen.

Used with permission. Copyright © Louise Morse August 2011
www.pilgrimsfriend.org.uk

@daily_encourage
We please God when we serve others.
Hannah Sarah Miles

SMILE:
'In the same way, after supper, he took the cup, gave thanks,
and broke it saying …'
Ministerial Blooper

41 WHAT'S SO GOOD? (GOOD FRIDAY)

Anna Drew writes: Good Friday – the day when Christians around the world pause to consider Jesus' betrayal, arrest, trial, execution and burial. Only one day to take in so much. So much sadness. So much confusion. So much grief. And ultimately so much disappointment. Perhaps it's only one day in the church calendar because that's as much as we could possibly cope with. This day closes with Jesus in the grave. I often wonder – what's so good about Good Friday?

In some ways, for Christians it's not so bad. After all, we know what's coming. We know that Jesus isn't dead forever. We know there is hope. It's easy to want to rush straight through Good Friday and Holy Saturday and on to Easter Sunday. We want to join Mary in the garden coming face to face with her Saviour and rushing back to tell the others 'He is Risen', 'Hallelujah'. We want to gorge ourselves on chocolate eggs and bask in the spring sunshine. We want to sing and dance and celebrate the joy of new life, sharing in the resurrection of our dear Messiah. But that wouldn't be right. That wouldn't be real. Not today. Today we stand at the graveside with the disciples. No one could really blame them for asking, 'What's so good about Good Friday?' He is *not* risen. He is dead. It seems that evil has won. Either Jesus was not the Messiah He claimed to be or He wasn't any kind of Messiah at all. For them it seemed the light had left the world. They stood in a place of utter hopelessness. Anyone who has ever grieved will feel something of their pain. Today, we come face to face with the costliness of the cross, the reality of sin and the depths of God's love. We see a God who takes sin seriously, but doesn't use it as a reason to abandon human beings. We see a God who takes sin so seriously that He would do anything to bring us back home.

A God who loves us so much He would go to the grave for us.

MAYBE TOMORROW you could take a quiet moment to stand at the graveside and consider the God who loves you this much.

Used with permission. Copyright © Anna Drew April 2011

NIGHT PRAYER:

'I'm sure now I'll see God's goodness in the exuberant earth. Stay with GOD! Take heart. Don't quit. I'll say it again: Stay with GOD.' (Psa. 27:13–14, *The Message*) Amen.

BIBLE READING:

'Jesus said, "It is finished." With that, he bowed his head and gave up his spirit.' **John 19:30**
Jesus' Crucifixion, Death and Burial **Luke 23:26–56**

FURTHER REFLECTION
BEING PATIENT ON HOLY SATURDAY:

Father God, Your Son, Jesus, wrapped in cloths after He was born
And laid in a wooden manger – vulnerable, but our living hope.
Today we think of the hopelessness of Jesus wrapped in the grave cloths
And laid in a tomb after being crucified on a cross – dead!
Holy God, forgive us!
Thank You, that on Easter Day, hope is born again with even greater power,
And strips of cloth are found lying by themselves
The Lord lives and lays dead no more – He is risen!
We praise You that He is now seated and crowned at Your right hand – clothed in Glory. Amen.
TM

@daily_encourage

Great Friday reminder: We live by faith and not by sight!

Hannah Sarah Miles

SMILE:

A poster read: 'God is dead' – Nietzsche. The graffiti underneath read: 'Nietzsche is dead' – God.

Anon.

HOPE FOR THE HOPELESS (EASTER DAY)

42

José Henriquez was a miner who'd spent thirty-seven years digging for gold and copper. In August 2010, whilst working 720 metres underground in the San Esteban mine in Chile, there was a huge explosion and a rock fall entombed him. Amazingly, José and his thirty-two co-workers survived. With barely any light, they found each other and gathered in an underground shelter. There was no way out and some panicked, not knowing if they'd live or die. They rationed their supplies to half a teaspoon of fish a day and some contaminated water. Even so, 54-year-old José believed God would rescue them. So he called his fellow miners together and pointed out that though it seemed as though they'd lost everything, they still had prayer! All of them started praying, even those who weren't Christians. We don't always get what we ask for when we pray, but their Bible readings and prayer kept their spirits up and they coped with darkness, hunger, thirst, and 32 degrees of heat.

When the first rescue drill came close, but missed them, they were devastated. They felt hopeless and wondered if their rescuers even knew they were alive. Yet after seventeen days, a second drill finally reached them and returned to the surface with a note reporting that all thirty-three were still alive! You can imagine the rejoicing above and deep beneath the earth. You probably remember the rest: how the world held its breath and waited another fifty-two days before 'The Phoenix' capsule was able to bring the miners to the surface. Then, after over two months, there was the incredible sight of the freed miners emerging one by one.

I heard José tell the unreported story at a church in Woodford, Essex. Astonishingly, despite their seemingly hopeless situation, at least twenty-two of the miners had become Christians whilst imprisoned. These Chileans proved that being trapped in a powerless situation doesn't have to imprison your soul. Faith in Jesus gave them new strength and hope. José spoke with joy of how their lives had been changed forever.

MAYBE TOMORROW the resurrection of Jesus can bring you hope, freedom and new life too. My neighbour and friend, Adrian Warnock, talks about the resurrection 'changing everything' in his excellent book *Raised with Christ*: 'It changed the cross from a tragedy into a triumph, and it changed the Roman Empire into a Christian state. This was the most powerful divine event in the history of creation, and it ushered in a new age of the Holy Spirit's activity and power in saving and transforming lives.'[17]

NIGHT PRAYER:

Living Lord Jesus, live within me, I pray. Complete Your saving work within me, and so transform me, that I may be an agent of Your light, hope and transformation in this dark and troubled world. Amen.

BIBLE READING:

St Paul said, 'For what I received I passed on to you as of first importance: that Christ died for our sins according to the Scriptures, that he was buried, that he was raised on the third day according to the Scriptures ...' **1 Corinthians 15:3–4**
The Resurrection **John 20:1–18**

FURTHER REFLECTION
BEING ALIVE IN CHRIST:

The secret to living for our heavenly Father isn't about knowing everything; it's about keeping close to Him.

It isn't about being perfect; it's recognising we're not and receiving forgiveness through the cross of Jesus.

It isn't about trying harder; it's trusting and following the Risen Christ – faithfully, obediently, one step at a time.

It isn't about what *we* can do, it's about what *He* can do gloriously in and through us – His Easter people!

@daily_encourage
Believe that God is the God of the impossible!

Hannah Sarah Miles

SMILE:

A Sunday school teacher had finished telling her primary school class how Jesus was crucified and placed in a tomb with a great stone sealing the opening. Then, wanting to share the excitement of the resurrection, she asked: 'And what do you think were Jesus' first words when He came bursting out of the tomb?' A little girl shot her hand up and leapt to her feet shouting excitedly, 'I know, I know!' 'Good,' said the teacher, 'Tell us Jesus' first words after He'd risen.' Extending her arms high into the air, she said: 'TA-DA!'

Anon.

BEING PREPARED

TOMORROW

Tomorrow is an X-Day, Lord,
an unknown quantity of unknown quality.
I'm not even sure that there will be a tomorrow.
      It's a might-be, not shall-be.
So far in my life sunrise has always followed sunset,
      but it won't always be so.

What does tomorrow conceal in its travelling bag?
      Joyous surprises?
      Let them all come.
      Good news?
      I'm thirsting for it.

Or there might possibly be sorrows …
      the death of a loved one?
If so, help me to be grateful for the hours we shared,
let memories bind a golden chain.
      Is sickness in the offing?
Let me learn lessons of patience and endurance.

Catastrophe may suddenly strike me:
      road accident?
      train wreck?
      air disaster?
      who knows?

Life has many ingredients, some good, some bad.
All kinds must come my way at some time.

Keep my heart steady, Lord, whatever tomorrow may bring.
Let me hold Your hand and walk unafraid with You;
For finally, Master, You will write one word

over my earthly life,
and that word will be
FINIS.

From Just A Moment Lord *by Flora Larsson, Published by Lakeland, Marshall Morgan Scott. Used with permission. Copyright © 1973 by The Salvation Army*

Jesus said 'You don't have to wait for the End. I am, right now, Resurrection and Life. The one who believes in me, even though he or she dies, will live. And everyone who lives believing in me does not ultimately die at all. Do you believe this?'
John 11:25–26, The Message

THROUGH THE YEAR 2

God sent His Son, they called Him Jesus;
He came to love, heal, and forgive;
He lived and died to buy my pardon,
An empty grave is there to prove my Saviour lives.

> *Because He lives I can face tomorrow;*
> *Because He lives all fear is gone;*
> *Because I know He holds the future,*
> *And life is worth the living*
> *Just because He lives.*

How sweet to hold a new-born baby,
And feel the pride and joy he gives;
But greater still the calm assurance,
This child can face uncertain days because He lives.
Refrain

And then one day I'll cross the river;
I'll fight life's final war with pain;
And then as death gives way to victory,
I'll see the lights of glory and I'll know He lives.
Refrain

William & Gloria Gaither, 'Bill' is an American Gospel singer and his wife, Gloria, has often written his lyrics Copyright © 1971 Gaither Music Company/ kingswaysongs.com: tym@kingsway.co.uk Used with permission.

PLAIN SAILING (PENTECOST)

43

I used to enjoy windsurfing (a damper version of sailing). To get anywhere, I'd have to put up the sail and catch the wind. If I didn't harness the wind's power, if I was impatient or went in the wrong direction, then I didn't get very far. The secret was allowing the wind to take me – working out how to make the best use of its power. When I did, I made progress. The wind sometimes took me in a straight line. At other times it was a longer route, involving a lot of tacking to and fro. Sometimes there was a gentle breeze and I needed a lot of patience to wait for the unexpected gust. But when it was really blowing, I'd have to cling on for dear life and see where it took me.

At Pentecost the wind of the Spirit blew upon the disciples. Until that moment they'd been feeling hopeless, wondering if they were going to get anywhere. Yet their fear and trembling were replaced by inspiration, power and confidence. Suddenly, they were on the move! It's interesting the Church is often symbolised as a boat. We're not all called to grab the rudder – steering the Church where we want it to go. Rather, we're called to grab oars together and row into God's windstream. Yet how do we catch the wind of the Spirit? Well, when we pray it's like putting up a sail – especially when we do so with an inner longing and willingness to receive from your heavenly Father. Discernment, endurance, and faithfulness are also necessary, together with an openness to surprises and new directions.

MAYBE TOMORROW you could be on the move too. Open your heart and pray for more of the life-giving breath of God. Trust God even when you've not seen much sign of His activity in your life or church. Be patient when there are the ripples of small beginnings. Then be expectant. Hold on tightly for the next gust.

NIGHT PRAYER:

Life-giving God, help me, together with my sisters and brothers in Christ, to catch the wind of Your Spirit. May Your Church bear fruit and exercise the gifts you give in love and with power. But now, may I rest and prepare myself for being used by You tomorrow. Amen.

BIBLE READING:

[Jesus said], 'The wind blows wherever it pleases. You hear its sound, but you cannot tell where it comes from or where it is going. So it is with everyone born of the Spirit.' **John 3:8**
Valley of dry bones **Ezekiel 37:1–14**

FURTHER REFLECTION
BEING A SPIRIT-LED DISCIPLE:

God does not always lead by the shortest route,
because some things are best learned on longer journeys.
God sometimes leads us into the wilderness,
as well as by still waters,
because some destinations are reached with scars as well as smiles.
God urges us to travel light,
but also to take things of our precious past with us,
because some things remind us where we've come from
and bring hope of a future.
God guides in different ways,
sometimes half-hidden, as in a grey cloud,
sometimes blazingly clear

because God's people are called to travel as God guides them, and there is never a time when God's guidance fails or ceases. As Jesus said, 'I am with you always.' Amen.

Used with permission. Copyright © Revd Dr Martyn Atkins September 2011

@daily_encourage

The Lord is at work in you and He will finish what He has begun.

Hannah Sarah Miles

SMILE:

God loves everyone, but probably prefers 'spiritual fruit' over 'religious nuts'!

Anon.

44 TO BE CONTINUED (ASCENSION)

I regularly work in the evenings, so it's a treat if I can get home early and flop in front of the TV. The trouble is, I often find myself getting stuck into an excellent programme that ends with, 'To be continued'. Frustrating because there might be a week until the next instalment! Worse still, inevitably I have a meeting when the second part is aired. Yes, iPlayer and recording facilities are a great help, but sometimes I forget to tune in after the wait.

Jesus' resurrection appearances could hardly just fizzle out. There had to be a climax – a time when His earthly ministry drew to a close. Yet the ascension wasn't a 'fait accompli'; it wasn't the end! Luke's Gospel tells us what Jesus 'began to do', whereas the Acts of the Apostles tells what happened next. The disciples couldn't stay on the mountaintop gazing into the sky; instead they had to go down into Jerusalem and wait obediently for the next instalment.

After Jesus had left them, He went to share His Father's throne and to send the Holy Spirit. Jesus was no longer limited by time or place: now He could be everywhere at once. Saint Augustine of Hippo, who was born around 300 years after Jesus' death, wrote, 'And [Jesus] departed from our sight, that we might return to our heart, and there find Him. For He departed, and behold, He is here' (*Confessions*, AD 397–98, Book 4, Chapter 12). He had to go to be more fully present. That presence can make a difference, if people fully receive and serve their King.

MAYBE TOMORROW you could ask: Am I expectantly waiting for Him to transform my life? Do I take seriously the fact that Jesus is my friend and Saviour, but also has authority over me as my Master and Lord?

NIGHT PRAYER:

Lord God, Alpha and Omega, at this day's end, prepare me for Your work to be continued tomorrow. Forgive my disobedience today. Be present in my heart by Your Spirit. Change me from within, so that I can be a witness to You as I share in Your mission and live the life You want for me. Amen.

BIBLE READING:

'In my former book, Theophilus, I wrote about all that Jesus began to do and to teach until the day he was taken up to heaven …' **Acts 1:1–2**
The Ascension **Luke 24:44–53**

FURTHER REFLECTION
BEING A DISCIPLE:

Loving Lord,
Thank you for all the many blessings you constantly bestow upon me.
Deepen and enrich my faith, as I look back in gratitude.
Enable me to move forward in faith as I face the challenges ahead.
Inspire me to reach out in love to others, especially those in need.
So may I walk in your way, and live to glorify your name. Amen.

Used with permission. Copyright © Revd Dr Peter Graves November 2011

'He cannot bless us unless he has us. When we try to keep within us an area that is our own, we try to keep an area of death. Therefore, in love, He claims all. There's no bargaining with Him.'[18]

Used with permission. C.S. Lewis – Scholar, novelist, and Christian apologist (1898–1963)

@daily_encourage

May you (yes you!) be blessed by the Lord, the Maker of heaven and earth. (Psa. 115:15)

Hannah Sarah Miles

SMILE:

'Heaven is much bigger than everything, than the whole universe. It has to be big to fit God and all the angels in. If God stood in front of us now I would probably only be able to see the bottom of his big toe.' Judy (child)

(From Dear God, Most Of The Time Your Quite Nice *– Maggie Durran)[19]*

COME, YE THANKFUL PEOPLE, GO! (HARVEST)

45

My wife Frances grew up in a Christian family and attended her local Methodist church. She remembers the collection plate being passed around each week and her minister offering it to God. As a small child, Frances actually thought that the money mysteriously went up to heaven as the minister lifted the plate. How cute! It's a lovely idea, but actually the money we offer to our heavenly Father remains in human hands. Amazingly, He entrusts us, via our church leaders and the wider Christian community, to use it to further His kingdom on earth. We're actually spending His money. All the more reason to do it prayerfully and carefully.

Harvest festivals are occasions when we collect more than just money. Gifts are often beautifully displayed at the front of church as a visual reminder that we've been blessed with the fruit of the earth. Such gifts inevitably include foodstuffs, flowers, and often these days, clothing and toiletries as well. They're offered in thankfulness for God's abundant provision and goodness. Yet, as with our money, these things are not magically taken up into heaven. Instead, it takes ordinary good-hearted people to share what's been given with those who need it most. Our harvest hymns should move us to action with our hands and feet, so that the love of Jesus is extended to the poor, the needy, the widow and the orphan. For me, Harvest time is a reminder I'm blessed and rich compared to many in the world. What's more, I'm also a caretaker: a steward of all that my Creator has entrusted to me. I should offer Him *everything* with thanksgiving – including what I keep, what I spend, and my time too.

MAYBE TOMORROW there's an organisation you could support that's seeking to relieve poverty – either in your community, or in a more distant part of the world. Out of gratitude to God, you could pray as you make the offering, and then metaphorically 'roll up your sleeves' and think 'Right, what can I do that's practical? Help them deliver? Support a foodbank?' It could pay dividends – not in money, but in your mood. For if we believe Jesus' words, 'There is more happiness in giving,' He said 'than in receiving' (Acts 20:35, GNB).

NIGHT PRAYER:

Lord Jesus, may the hymns of praise I sing move me to action. Help me to recognise my response-ability, for the sake of Your kingdom. Amen.

BIBLE READING:

'He has shown all you people what is good. And what does the LORD require of you? To act justly and to love mercy and to walk humbly with your God.' **Micah 6:8, TNIV**
Boaz helps a foreigner at harvest time **Ruth 2**

FURTHER REFLECTION
BEING THANKFUL FOR GOD'S PROMISES:

In the midst of hunger and war
 We celebrate the promise of plenty and peace.

In the midst of oppression and tyranny
 We celebrate the promise of service and freedom.

In the midst of doubt and despair
 We celebrate the promise of faith and hope.

In the midst of fear and betrayal
We celebrate the promise of joy and happiness.

In the midst of hatred and death
We celebrate the promise of love and life.

In the midst of sin and decay
We celebrate the promise of Salvation and renewal.

In the midst of death on every side
We celebrate the promise of the living Christ. Amen.

Used with permission. The Iona Community [20]

@daily_encourage

Focus on what God has done for you, rather than what He
has not. Remember we are here to serve God. Not the other
way round!

Hannah Sarah Miles

SMILE:
What do you call someone who *used* to be really keen on
farmyard vehicles? An ex-tractor fan!

Anon.

46 GRANDAD'S BIBLE (REMEMBRANCE)

My grandad died aged 94, but he shouldn't have lived to be older than 28! He was a paratrooper during the war in the Sixth Airborne Regiment – a 'Red Beret'. Seven British planes and some US aircraft were flying to the Rhine, because the Germans were supposed to be away fighting the Russians – except they weren't, so most of the British paratroopers got ambushed as they landed. My grandad's parachute jump went OK, but on the ground, whilst he was looking for his radio equipment, a bomb exploded. As Grandad lay dying, two German women found him almost unconscious in a field. They couldn't understand a word he was saying. Yet these ordinary ladies bravely took him to a British medical tent, where a female surgeon operated on him – literally 'in the field'. He then got sent to Holland, and eventually to an English hospital for six months. 'I'm a lucky man, Tony,' he said to me once. Grandad spent the rest of his life in pain, full of shrapnel, metal splinters breaking through his skin – including a big lump that turned out to be a bullet. He owed his life to two people who saw a suffering human being, rather than the 'enemy'. He never forgot them.

Grandad didn't like acts of remembrance. He preferred to try and forget the war and losing so many friends. He'd rather be left alone with his thoughts. I've never even seen his medals. However, the amazing thing was, he wasn't screwed up with anger at any particular person – only at the futility of war itself. 'Blessed are the peacemakers,' Jesus said.

Grandad left me something that meant a lot to him: his little blue Bible that every soldier got from King George VI. Unbelievably, it travelled with him through all the horrors, and survived too. But it's no good my just having it. I need to read it, then let the words change me and my attitude towards others.

MAYBE TOMORROW is a day to take on the wise words of a Jesuit priest: 'If it's peace you want, seek to change yourself, not other people. It's easier to protect your feet with slippers, than to carpet the whole Earth.' (Anthony de Mello)

NIGHT PRAYER:

Thank You, Lord, for Grandad and his fellow soldiers. Tonight I pray that You will help the heroes who seek to keep or make peace today and everyone who has been affected by past and present world conflicts. Amen.

BIBLE READING:

Jesus said, 'My command is this: Love each other as I have loved you. Greater love has no one than this: to lay down one's life for one's friends.' **John 15:12–13, TNIV**
'... and he began to teach them, saying: "Blessed are the poor in spirit, for theirs is the kingdom of heaven ... Blessed are they who hunger and thirst for righteousness, for they will be filled. Blessed are the merciful, for they will be shown mercy. Blessed are the pure in heart for they will see God. Blessed are the peacemakers, for they will be called sons of God ..."' **Matthew 5:1–12**

FURTHER REFLECTION
WASTE:

Waste of Muscle, waste of Brain,
Waste of Patience, waste of Pain,
Waste of Manhood, waste of Health,
Waste of Beauty, waste of Wealth,
Waste of Blood, and waste of Tears,
Waste of Youth's most precious years,
Waste of ways the Saints have trod,
Waste of Glory, waste of God – War!

Padre Geoffrey A. Studdert Kennedy (1883–1929), known as 'Woodbine Willie' – the soldiers' friend.[21]

@daily_encourage

Turn to God when fear tells you to turn around.

Hannah Sarah Miles

SMILE:

The church will host an evening of fine dining, superb entertainment, and gracious hostility.

Church Bulletin Blooper – Anon.

COMING ... READY OR NOT! (ADVENT)

47

A little girl quizzed her mother after learning about the second coming in Sunday school. 'Mummy, do you believe Jesus will come back?' 'Yes, I do,' said Mum. 'Could He come this week?' 'Yes,' Mum echoed. 'Today?' the girl asked in amazement. 'Yep,' Mum confirmed. 'Could He come in the next hour?' 'Indeed He could.' 'In a few minutes?' 'Yes, dear.' Then, after a pause ... 'Mummy, would you comb my hair?'

Like Lent, Advent should be a time of anticipation and preparation. We remember there's a past, present and future to our understanding of how Jesus comes to us: at Christmas we remember the incredible fact that the Son of God *was* born in Bethlehem as a baby – to be God with Us! So, we prepare to celebrate Christmas. Then Christians believe Jesus comes into our lives through the Holy Spirit *today* – Christ at work within us. So we should invite Him to fill our hearts each day. But there's also clear teaching in the Bible that one day Jesus will come again – to be our judge. In all three senses Jesus comes ... whether we are ready, or not. He gives 'signs' to warn us, but the exact time of His second coming to us is unknown. Dr Stephen H. Travis once said that the signs that we read about in the Bible 'are not like the signs which say, "End of Motorway 1 mile". They are in fact more like the hazard warning lights which warn us of dangers along the way.'[22] All we know is our journey has a purpose and history is going somewhere. There lies our hope, but also a challenge. Have we let the journey lull us to sleep, or are we actually ready – vigilant and faithful?

When Jesus came for the first time, He took people by surprise and they weren't ready for Him. We busily prepare for Christmas in so many ways today, but it could be that much of our preparation is misdirected. Those things you consider important – would He? Remember, it's too late to prepare for an examination when the paper is before you!

MAYBE TOMORROW you could consider whether or not you are ready for the coming of Jesus. Every year Bishop Charles Gore (1853–1932) used to preach to candidates on the night before their Ordination. His sermon would always conclude with the same challenge: 'Tomorrow I shall say to you, wilt thou, wilt thou, wilt thou? But there will come a day to you when another will say to you, hast thou, hast thou, hast thou?'

NIGHT PRAYER:

I am full of good intentions, Lord. Forgive me when I don't live up to them, and help me to change. I am sleepy now, so please help me rest well, that I may be fully awake tomorrow and more ready for Your coming. Amen.

BIBLE READING:

[Jesus said], 'But about that day or hour no one knows, not even the angels in heaven, nor the Son, but only the Father. Be on guard! Be alert! You do not know when that time will come.'
Mark 13:32–33, TNIV
Like a thief in the night **1 Thessalonians 5:1–11**

FURTHER REFLECTION
BEING WELCOMING:

Lord Jesus, we know you want to come to us,
to be born in us, to live with us,
so please help us to make room for you.
Help us to make room in our hearts,
so they may be filled with your love.

Help us to make room in our minds,
so they may be filled with your wisdom.
Help us to make room in our busy schedules,
so our time may be filled with your peace.
Help us to make room in our homes,
so they may be filled with your presence.
Help us to make room in our economies,
so they may be filled with your generosity.
Help us to make room in our prejudices, that we may recognise
you when you come to us in the form of the stranger, the poor,
the hungry and the naked.
For this we ask humbly and in your name. Amen.

Used with permission. Copyright © Revd Dr Janet Corlett 2011

@daily_encourage

You may be waiting on God. Don't give up! He acts in His
own timing and may surprise you. Maybe there'll be a
surprise tomorrow.

Hannah Sarah Miles

SMILE:

A woman went to the post office to buy some stamps for her
Christmas cards. 'What denomination?' asked the assistant
at the counter. 'What? I can't believe it has come to this!' said
the woman. 'Well, you'd better give me 50 Methodist and 50
Catholic ones.'

Anon.

48 HAVE A CRACKING CHRISTMAS (CHRISTMAS EVE/DAY)

The pulling of Christmas crackers goes back to the early 1840s. Tom Smith, a baker and confectioner, started wrapping 'bon bons' in tissue paper with mottos inside. Later, when he heard the crackle after throwing a log on a fire, Tom had an idea that grew into the crackers we use today. I'm sure he didn't intend them to speak of the good news of Jesus. But every cracker has a gift, crown, smile (joke), and a spark:

THE GIFT: God so loved, that He GAVE Jesus, He's the gift at the heart of Christmas – but not a cheap short-lived novelty.
THE CROWN: Jesus was a different kind of king – the KING of Love who wore a crown of thorns and died to save us.
THE SMILE: The JOY of the Lord comes through His resurrection and the new life He makes possible.
THE SPARK: After Jesus ascended into heaven, He sent the FIRE of His Holy Spirit to help, comfort and empower us.
And remember we can't pull a cracker alone, TEAMWORK is required: We must help each other if we're to make progress.

MAYBE TOMORROW you could explore these ideas and talk about them when you pull your crackers and eat your meal – especially if you have non-Christian friends at the table. Jesus has been marginalised right from His birth in Bethlehem. Many enjoy seasonal celebrations and food, family and friends, but sadly relatively few will pause to remember that 'Christmas Starts with Christ'.[23] I hope your Christmas crackers will become visual aids and conversation starters. Oh, and don't forget to say 'Grace' and pray for those who are not as fortunate as you are.

NIGHT PRAYER:

Thank You that Jesus never gives up on me and on all those He came to save. Amen.

BIBLE READING:

'For God so loved the world that he gave his one and only Son, that whoever believes in him shall not perish but have eternal life.' **John 3:16**
The Birth of Jesus **Luke 2:1–7**

FURTHER REFLECTION
BEING BORN IN A STINKING MESS:

To a young couple far from home
God broke into the world
Recognised by some, ignored by many

Born into an occupied land
Frightened shepherds heard angels sing
God broke into the world
Surprising those who heard the message

Born a Jew
Wise men from the East came to visit
God broke into the world
Keeping away from kings and palaces

Born for us today
To all who will hear and respond
God breaks into our hearts and lives
Disturbing, challenging, transforming
Emmanuel: God is with us.

Used with permission. Copyright © Deacon Eunice Atwood January 2010

@daily_encourage

A child is born to us, a son is given to us. The government will rest on his shoulders (Isa. 9:6). ☺ love H. x

Hannah Sarah Miles

SMILE:

A four-year-old boy was asked to give thanks before Christmas dinner. Everyone bowed heads in expectation. He began his prayer thanking God for all his friends, naming them one by one. Then he thanked God for Mummy and Daddy, brother and sister, Grandma and Grandpa, and all his aunts and uncles. Then he began to thank God for the food. He gave thanks for the turkey, the dressing, the fruit salad, the cranberry sauce, the pies, the cakes and even the custard. Then he paused … and everyone waited … and waited. After a long silence, he looked up at his mother and asked, 'If I thank God for the sprouts, won't He know I'm lying?'

Anon.

A TOUGH RESOLUTION (NEW YEAR)

49

On many occasions, including the 25 December 1747, John Wesley fervently encouraged the 'Methodists' in the movement he founded to renew their covenant (a binding promise) with God. It has become a sort of New Year's resolution for the Methodist Church and part of a serious and extremely challenging service. For me, it's an opportunity to thank God for the past, make a fresh commitment to serve Jesus, and publicly express the intention to follow Him in the year ahead with my Christian sisters and brothers. The service includes this very tough prayer – a sign of our commitment to loving trust, and obedience:

I am no longer my own but yours.
Put me to what you will, rank me with whom you will;
put me to doing, put me to suffering;
let me be employed for you, or laid aside for you,
exalted for you, or brought low for you;
let me be full, let me be empty,
let me have all things, let me have nothing:
I freely and wholeheartedly yield all things to your pleasure and disposal.
And now, glorious and blessed God,
Father, Son and Holy Spirit, you are mine and I am yours.
So be it. And the covenant made on earth, let it be ratified in heaven. Amen.

Used with permission. Copyright © Trustees for Methodist Church Purposes

MAYBE TOMORROW I will be better able to live for God
and others, and not just for my rights and myself.

NIGHT PRAYER:

God of the ages,
You are before us, with us and beyond us.
Lead us, we pray, from winter to spring; from night to day;
from darkness to light;
from slumber to consciousness; from an old year to a
new beginning.
May Your renewing Spirit burst forth into our lives
with forgiveness, fresh vision, and blessed hope;
through the resurrecting power of our Lord Jesus Christ.
Amen.

BIBLE READING:

'Do not conform to the pattern of this world, but be
transformed by the renewing of your mind. Then you will be
able to test and approve what God's will is – his good, pleasing
and perfect will.' **Romans 12:2 (NIV, 2011)**
A New Covenant **Jeremiah 31:31–34**

FURTHER REFLECTION
BEING HOPEFUL:

Lord, we sometimes sing a hymn which starts 'Lord of all
hopefulness, Lord of all joy.'
In a world where there is so much hopelessness, help me to
bring Your love into other people's lives so that they might
know You the 'Lord of all hopefulness'. To people who feel
themselves hopeless, help me to show them that You created
each person for a purpose and that in You there is fulfilment
and meaning for their lives. To those who find themselves in
seemingly hopeless situations, give me wisdom to help them see

the way through to victory.
Lord, wherever there is 'less' than Your best please bring
Your 'fullness'.
Restore HOPE to Your needy world. Amen.

Used with permission. Copyright © Linda Ashford October 2011
www.hopetogether.org.uk

@daily_encourage

Someone once said 'HOPE' is Holding On Praying Expectantly!

Hannah Sarah Miles

SMILE:

The optimist is wrong as often as the pessimist. But he has a lot
more fun.

Anon.

50 THE PASSAGE
HELPING HOMELESS PEOPLE

My final thought I leave you with is a challenge in the form of a letter from Mick Clarke of The Passage, a charity for the homeless.

St Vincent's Centre
Carlisle Place
London SW1P 1NL

Tel: 020 7592 1850
Fax: 020 7592 1870
info@passage.org.uk
www.passage.org.uk

The Passage was set up in 1980 by Cardinal Basil Hume and the Daughters of Charity (a religious order) in response to the number of people sleeping out on the streets of Victoria, Westminster, in London. Since then we have helped over 100,000 people affected by homelessness and now run the largest Resource Centre for homeless people in the UK, offering diverse services (from food, clothing, and showers to street outreach, health care and employment and education services) to meet a range of complex needs, as well as running accommodation and community projects.

At The Passage we take our values from the work of Vincent De Paul, a Christian and social reformer from the seventeenth century, who took the words spoken by Jesus in Matthew 25:40 ('in so far as you do this to one of the least of these brothers of mine, you do it to me', NJB) as inspiration to live out the Gospel. Vincent's Christian vocation demanded he work with those who are most vulnerable and downtrodden. He believed God is present in each of them and that they should be treated with the respect and love their God-given individuality demands.

Vincent also believed in lasting, not short-term change. Today The Passage works towards lasting change (not short-term fixes) for our clients; addressing the root causes that have led to their homelessness in the first place (addiction, mental health issues, etc), so that the cycle of their homelessness can be broken once and for all.

A good example of this approach is James. James first met The Passage when on the streets sleeping out; his drinking had led to him losing his job, his home and his family. James felt that he 'had lost it all'. After being encouraged to use the Resource Centre services by one of our street workers, James was found accommodation in a Passage project and linked into Passage services to address his addiction. Now, after three years of being alcohol-free, James has his own flat, is working and (at weekends) gets to spend time with his children; lasting, not short-term change.

Every Good Friday The Passage takes part in a traditional 'walk of witness' in the Victoria area, commencing at Methodist Central Hall, pausing at Westminster Cathedral and culminating at Westminster Abbey. One year, as the procession was about to leave, one Passage client (who led the procession by carrying a large cross) turned to one of the Passage workers (who had gone to help them get ready to move off) and said, 'Are you here to help me carry my cross?' It is a good description of the work of our work at The Passage: indeed, the work we are all called to, in our own individual vocation, whatever that may be.

Mick Clarke
Chief Executive, The Passage
www.passage.org.uk
To make a donation: 0845 880 0689

HELPING HOMELESS PEOPLE FOR 30 YEARS
FOUNDING PATRON Cardinal Basil Hume
PATRON Archbishop Vincent Nichols

CLOSING REFLECTION

Dear God and Father of humanity,
Homelessness hurts when there are
Too many people and too few rooms;
But I believe You are there, Lord.
Homelessness hurts when there is
No work, no home and no room;
But You are there.
Homelessness hurts in the fear,
the loneliness and the dark of the night,
The sharpness of the street and the cold of the concrete;
But that is where You are tonight.
Almighty Father, be present to me this night;
Heal the hurts of Your people,
And call us to build Your kingdom. Amen.

*Used with permission. Copyright © Father Padraig Regan –
Chaplain to The Passage. January 2012*

PRAYERS, TEXTS AND HYMNS FOR NIGHT-TIME

While I sleep, O Lord,
let my heart not cease to worship you;
fill my sleep with your presence,
while creation itself keeps watch,
singing psalms with the angels,
and taking up my soul into its paean of praise.

St Gregory of Nazianzus – Archbishop of Constantinople –
aka 'Gregory the Theologian' (c.330–389)

Almighty God, help me to keep close to Jesus,
especially through our prayer and devotions.
May I lean upon my Lord and listen.
Help me to hear His heartbeat
and live confidently knowing that He is my Living Saviour.
Guide me that I might live in a way that is in harmony with
Your Holy Spirit
and NOT dance to the world's tune.
Rather, release me to discover Your holy rhythm of life.
Then, as I let the Lord of the dance lead me,
may my steps take me through the difficult places
to the place of Your glory, peace and eternal joy.
I ask this in the name of my companion and Lord. Amen.
TM

Bless this house and those within
Bless our giving and receiving
Bless our words and conversation
Bless our hands and recreation
Bless our sowing and our growing
Bless our coming and our going
Bless all who enter and depart
Bless this house, your peace impart
Used with permission. © John Birch www.faithandworship.com

Come, Lord,
And cover me with the night.
Spread your grace over us
As you assured us you would do.

Your promises are more than
All the stars in the sky;
Your mercy is deeper than the night.
Lord, it will be cold.

The night comes with its breath of death.
Night comes; the end comes; you come.

Lord, we wait for you
Day and night.

Ghana

Come now, turn aside for a while from your daily employment,
escape for a moment from the tumult of your thoughts.
Put aside your weighty cares, let your burdensome distractions
wait,
free yourself for a while for God and rest awhile in him.
Enter the inner chamber of your soul,
shut out everything except God and that which can help you in
seeking him,
and when you have shut the door, seek him.
Now, my soul, say to God, 'I seek your face; Lord it is your face
that I seek.' Amen.

*St Anselm of Canterbury – Italian clergyman, scholastic philosopher and
theologian (1033–1109)*

Jesus said, 'Come to me, all you who are weary and burdened,
and I will give you rest.'

Matthew 11:28

Eternal Spirit, living God
In whom I live and love and have my being
All that I am, have been and shall be is known to You.
You know the very secrets of my heart,
All that is within me that troubles and disturbs my peace.
For Lord, it is night again and the day is over.
May I rest in You
and be still in the presence of You, my God.

I offer to You the day that has been
What has been done – has been done
What has not been done, has not been done
May I let it be.
Living Flame, burn into me
Cleansing Wind, blow through me
Fountain of Water, well up within me.
Let the quietness of Your peace enfold me
And those dear to me.
As the night waits for the dawn
Let me look to the new day
With its new joys and new possibilities
In expectation of meeting You in it.
In Christ I pray, Amen.

Used with permission. Copyright © Deacon Denise Creed August 2011

Flood my soul, O God, with Your presence.
Penetrate my whole being with Your Spirit.
Shine through me with Your light.
May others look into my life
and see only their Lord and Saviour, Jesus Christ. Amen.

*Venerable John Henry Cardinal Newman – Convert to Roman Catholicism
from Anglicanism (1801–1890)*

Go with each of us to rest;
If any awake,
temper to them the dark hours of watching;
and when the day returns,
return to us, our sun and comforter,
and call us up with morning faces
and with morning hearts, eager to labour,
eager to be happy, if happiness should be our portion,
and if the day be marked for sorrow, strong to endure it.

Robert Louis Stevenson – Scottish novelist, essayist, and poet (1850–1894)

God of the day and of the night,
in me there is darkness, but with you there is light.
I am alone, but you will not leave me.
I am weak, but you will come to my help.
I am restless, but you are my peace.
I am in haste, but you are the God of infinite patience.
I am confused and lost, but you are eternal wisdom and you
direct my path; now and for ever. Amen

*Dietrich Bonhoeffer – German Lutheran pastor, theologian, musician, and martyr
(1906–1945).* Letters and Papers from Prison, *SCM Translation 1979 © SCM Press.
Used by permission of Hymns Ancient and Modern Ltd.*

God to enfold me,
God to surround me,
God in my speaking,
God in my thinking.
God in my sleeping,
God in my waking,
God in my watching,
God in my hoping.
God in my life,
God in my lips,
God in my soul,
God in my heart.
God in my sufficing,
God in my slumber,
God in mine ever-living soul,
God in mine eternity.

*Ancient Celtic Oral traditions – Carmina Gadelica, hymns and incantations
translated by amateur folklorist Alexander Carmichael (1832–1912)
in the Gaelic-speaking regions of Scotland between 1855 and 1910.*

He who dwells in the shelter of the Most High
will rest in the shadow of the Almighty.
I will say of the LORD, 'He is my refuge and my fortress,
my God, in whom I trust.'

Surely he will save you from the fowler's snare and from the
deadly pestilence.
He will cover you with his feathers, and under his wings you
will find refuge;
his faithfulness will be your shield and rampart.
You will not fear the terror of night, nor the arrow that flies by day,
nor the pestilence that stalks in the darkness, nor the plague
that destroys at midday.
A thousand may fall at your side, ten thousand at your right
hand, but it will not come near you.
You will only observe with your eyes and see the punishment of
the wicked.
If you make the Most High your dwelling – even the LORD, who
is my refuge –
then no harm will befall you, no disaster will come near your tent.
For he will command his angels concerning you to guard you
in all your ways;
they will lift you up in their hands, so that you will not strike
your foot against a stone.
You will tread upon the lion and the cobra; you will trample
the great lion and the serpent.
'Because he loves me,' says the LORD, 'I will rescue him;
I will protect him, for he acknowledges my name.
He will call upon me, and I will answer him; I will be with him
in trouble, I will deliver him and honour him. With long life
will I satisfy him and show him my salvation.'

Psalm 91

Into your hands, O Lord, we commend our souls and bodies,
beseeching you to keep us this night under your protection and
to strengthen us for our service tomorrow, for Christ's sake.
Amen.

*William Laud – Archbishop of Canterbury from 1633 and beheaded during the
English Civil War (1753–1645)*

I hear no voice, I feel no touch,
I see no glory bright;
But yet I know that God is near,
In darkness as in light.
He watches ever by my side,
And hears my whispered prayer:
The Father for His little child
Both night and day doth care.

Child's evening prayer – Anon.

I lift up my eyes to the hills – where does my help come from?
My help comes from the LORD, the Maker of heaven and earth.
He will not let your foot slip – he who watches over you will
not slumber;
indeed, he who watches over Israel will neither slumber nor sleep.
The LORD watches over you – the LORD is your shade at your
right hand;
the sun will not harm you by day, nor the moon by night.
The LORD will keep you from all harm – he will watch over
your life;
the LORD will watch over your coming and going both now and
forevermore.

Psalm 121

Know that the LORD has set apart the godly for himself;
the LORD will hear when I call to him.
In your anger do not sin;
when you are on your beds,
search your hearts and be silent.
Offer right sacrifices and trust in the LORD.
Many are asking, 'Who can show us any good?'
Let the light of your face shine upon us, O LORD.
You have filled my heart with greater joy
than when their grain and new wine abound.

I will lie down and sleep in peace,
for you alone, O LORD, make me dwell in safety.
Psalm 4

May the God of peace bring peace to this house
May the Son of peace bring peace to this house
May the Spirit of peace bring peace to this house
this night and all nights

Used with permission. © John Birch www.faithandworship.com

My soul finds rest in God alone;
my salvation comes from him.
He alone is my rock and my salvation;
he is my fortress, I will never be shaken.

Psalm 62:1–2

Now I lay me down to sleep,
I pray the Lord my soul to keep:
May God guard me through the night
And wake me with the morning light. Amen.

Traditional – Anon.

Now that the sun has set,
I sit and rest, and think of you.
Give my weary body peace.
Let my legs and arms stop aching,
Let my nose stop sneezing,
Let my head stop thinking.
Let me sleep in your arms.

African Dinka Prayer

O Lord, support us all the day long,
until the shadows lengthen,
and the evening comes,
and the busy world is hushed,
and the fever of life is over,
and our work is done.
Then in your mercy,
grant us a safe lodging and a holy rest,
and peace at the last. Amen.

Venerable John Henry Cardinal Newman – Convert to Roman Catholicism from Anglicanism (1801–1890)

One of those days Jesus went out to a mountainside to pray, and spent the night praying to God.

Luke 6:12

Rejoice in the Lord always. I will say it again: Rejoice!
Let your gentleness be evident to all. The Lord is near.
Do not be anxious about anything, but in every situation,
by prayer and petition, with thanksgiving, present your
requests to God.
And the peace of God, which transcends all understanding,
will guard your hearts and your minds in Christ Jesus.

Philippians 4:4–7 (NIV, 2011)

Send your peace into my heart, O Lord,
that I may be contented with the mercies of this day
and confident of your protection for this night;
and having forgiven others, even as you forgive me,
may I go to rest in tranquileity and trust;
through Jesus Christ our Lord.

St Francis of Assisi – Roman Catholic friar and founder of the Order of the Friars Minor, known as the Franciscans (1182–1226)

The sleep of a labourer is sweet, whether they eat little or much,
but as for the rich, their abundance permits them no sleep.

Ecclesiastes 5:12 (NIV, 2011)

To my weariness, O Lord, grant Your rest;
To my exhaustion, your strength and to my tired eyes, Your
Healing light.
Guide me, guard me and shelter me within the shadow of
Your wings
and quicken me in Your service with the brightness of Your glory;
Through Christ our Lord. Amen.

Lancelot Andrewes – English Bishop and scholar (1555–1626)

Watch, dear Lord,
with those who wake, or watch, or weep tonight,
and give Your angels charge over those who sleep.
Tend Your sick ones, O Lord Christ,
Rest Your weary ones,
Bless Your dying ones.
Soothe Your suffering ones.
Pity Your afflicted ones.
Shield Your joyous ones.
And all for Your Love's sake. Amen.

St Augustine of Hippo – influential Christian thinker, philosopher/theologian (354–430)

Why is this night so dark
that even the street light outside my window
can only cast black shadows
over the bed where I lie
counting dark seconds,
numbering the minutes, the hours
before daybreak?

PRAYERS, TEXTS AND HYMNS FOR NIGHT-TIME

Where are you God when I need you?
Too busy watching the psalmist
sit down, stand up while you make
his enemies into footstools?
When will you deal with my enemies,
turn my despair into furniture?
When will you lighten my dark?

Let me close my eyes, God,
shut out the dark, rest
my head on a pillow of sleep.
Let there be light when I awake
and a letter, a phone call
from someone I love.

Oh God, my God, God of the night,
God of the day: do not forget me.

Used with permission. Copyright © Kaye Lee January 2012

ADDITIONAL HYMNS

And now another day is gone
I'll sing my Maker's praise,
I'll sing my Maker's praise.
My comforts every hour make known
His providence and grace
His providence and grace.

I lay my body down to sleep
May angels guard my head
May angels guard my head,
And through the hours of darkness keep
Their watch around my bed
Their watch around my bed.

With cheerful heart I close my eyes
Since I may trust your love
Since I may trust your love,
And in the morning let me rise
Rejoicing in your love
Rejoicing in your love.

Isaac Watts – English preacher, theologian and hymn writer (1674–1748)

Glory to thee, my God, this night
For all the blessings of the light;
Keep me, O keep me, King of kings,
Beneath thine own almighty wings.

Forgive me, Lord, for thy dear Son,
The ill that I this day have done,
That with the world, myself, and thee,
I, ere I sleep, at peace may be.

Teach me to live, that I may dread
The grave as little as my bed;
Teach me to die, that so I may
Rise glorious at the judgement day.

O may my soul on thee repose,
And may sweet sleep mine eyelids close–
Sleep that shall me more vigorous make
To serve my God when I awake.

When in the night I sleepless lie,
My mind with heavenly thoughts supply;
Let no ill dreams disturb my rest,
No powers of darkness me molest.

Praise God, from whom all blessings flow;
Praise him, all creatures here below;
Praise him, above, ye heavenly host;
Praise Father, Son, and Holy Ghost.

Bishop Thomas Ken – Anglican clergyman (1637–1711)

The day thou gavest, Lord, is ended,
The darkness falls at thy behest;
To thee our morning hymns ascended,
Thy praise shall sanctify our rest.

We thank thee that thy church unsleeping,
While earth rolls onward into light,
Through all the world her watch is keeping,
And rests not now by day or night.

As o'er each continent and island
The dawn leads on another day,
The voice of prayer is never silent,
Nor dies the strain of praise away.

The sun that bids us rest is waking
Our brethren 'neath the western sky,
And hour by hour fresh lips are making
Thy wondrous doings heard on high.

So be it, Lord; thy throne shall never,
Like earth's proud empires, pass away;
Thy kingdom stands, and grows for ever,
Till all thy creatures own thy sway.

John Ellerton – hymn writer and hymnologist (1826–1893)

For all who watch tonight,
By land or sea or air,
O Father, may they know that Thou
Art with them even there.

For all who weep tonight,
The hearts that cannot rest,
Reveal Thy love, that wondrous love
Which gave for us Thy best.

For all who wake tonight,
Love's tender watch to keep,
Watcher divine, Thyself draw nigh,
Thou who dost never sleep.

For all who fear tonight,
Whate'er the dread may be,
We ask for them the perfect peace
Of hearts that rest in Thee.

Our own beloved tonight,
O Father, keep; and where
Our love and succour cannot reach,
Now bless them through our prayer.

And all who pray tonight,
Thy wrestling hosts, O Lord,
Make weakness strong, let them prevail,
According to Thy word.

Constance Coote – wife of an Anglican clergyman and eventual baronet (1844–1936)
Metre: SM

God will take care of you: all through the day
Jesus is near you to keep you from ill;
Waking or resting, at work or at play,
Jesus is with you, and watching you still.
He will take care of you: all through the night
Jesus, the Shepherd, His little one keeps;
Darkness to Him is the same as the light;
He never slumbers, and He never sleeps.

He will take care of you: all through the year,
Crowning each day with His kindness and love,
Sending you blessings, and shielding from fear,
Leading you on to the bright home above.

He will take care of you: yes, to the end:
Nothing can alter His love for His own;
Children, be glad that you have such a Friend;
He will not leave you one moment alone.

Frances Ridley Havergal – English poet and hymn writer (1836–1879)

Now God be with us, for the night is closing,
The light and darkness are of his disposing,
And 'neath his shadow here to rest we yield us,
For he will shield us.

Let evil thoughts and spirits flee before us;
Till morning cometh, watch, Protector, o'er us;

In soul and body thou from harm defend us;
Thine angels send us.

Let our last thoughts be thine when sleep o'ertakes us;
Our earliest thoughts be thine when morning wakes us;
All day serve thee, in all that we are doing.
Thy praise pursuing.

We have no refuge, none on earth to aid us,
Save thee, O Father, who thine own hast made us;
But thy dear presence will not leave them lonely,
Who seek thee only.

Father, thy name be praised, thy kingdom given,
Thy will be done on earth as 'tis in heaven;
Keep us in life, forgive our sins, deliver
Us now and ever.

*Die Nacht ist kommen, drin wir ruhen sollen, Petrus Herbert (fl.1566), translated
by Catherine Winkworth (1827–1878)*

Round me falls the night;
Saviour, be my light;
through the hours in darkness shrouded
let me see thy face unclouded;
let thy glory shine
in this heart of mine.

Earthly work is done,
earthly sounds are none;
rest in sleep and silence seeking,
let me hear thee softly speaking;
in my spirit's ear
whisper, 'I am near.'

Blessèd, heavenly Light,
shining through earth's night;
voice, that oft of love hast told me;
arms, so strong to clasp and hold me;
thou thy watch wilt keep,
Saviour, o'er my sleep.

William Romanis – Anglican clergyman and hymn writer (1824–1899)

Through the day your love has spared us,
Now as we lie down to rest,
Through the silent watches guard us,
Let no foe our peace molest;
Jesus, never-failing light,
May we rest in you tonight.

Pilgrims here on earth and strangers,
Dwelling in the midst of foes,
Us and ours preserve from dangers,
In your arms may we repose;
Jesus, when our days are past,
May we rest with you at last.

Thomas Kelly – Irish hymn writer (1769–1854)

Ye that have spent the silent night
In sleep and quiet rest,
And joy to see the cheerful light
That riseth in the east;
Now lift your hearts, your voices raise,
Your morning tribute bring,
And pay a grateful song of praise `
To heaven's almighty king.

And as this gloomy night did last
But for a little space;
As heavenly day, now night is past,
Doth show his pleasant face:
So let us hope, when faith and love
Their work on earth have done,
God's blessed face to see above,
Heaven's better, brighter sun.

God grant us grace that height to gain,
That glorious sight to see,
And send us, after worldly pain,
A life from trouble free;
Where cheerful day shall ever shine,
And sorrow never come:
Lord, be a place, a portion mine,
In that bright blissful home.

George Gascoigne – English poet and translator (c.1525–1577)

NOTES

RHYTHM AND REST

1. Sylvia Maddox, www.explorefaith.org Article: 'Where can I touch the edge of heaven?' 2004.
2. Referring to the Transfiguration cf. Matthew 17:1–9 Mark 9:2–8; and Luke 9:28–36.
3. Steve Jobs, speech given at Stanford University.
4. C.S. Lewis, *Surprised by Joy* (Harvest Books, 1966).
5. C.S. Lewis, *Mere Christianity*, Copyright © C.S. Lewis Pte. Ltd. 1942, 1943, 1944, 1952. Used with permission.
6. Tony Schwartz, *The Way We're Working Isn't Working* (London: Simon & Schuster, 2010) p.281.
7. Ibid. pp.63–66.
8. The Cooper Center Longitudinal Study. www.cooperinstitute.org/ccls
9. Brian Draper runs Echosounder, an enterprise that works with leaders and organisations to nurture their spiritual intelligence. Author of *Spiritual Intelligence* (Oxford: Lion Hudson, 2009).
10. Tony Schwartz, op.cit. pp.49–50.

PEACE AND JOY

11. Richard Rohr, *Falling Upward* (San Francisco: Jossey-Bass, Wiley, 2011) p.ix.

LOVING AND SERVING

12. Adapted from Tony and Frances Miles, *Like A Child* (Loughton, Essex: Rooftops Publishing, 2003) p.126.

TRIALS AND TRAUMAS

13. Derek Dobson, *Aspirations* (Bromley: Runnymede Publishing, 1998) p.77.
14. Tony Schwartz, op. cit. p.177f.
15. Adapted from Tony and Frances Miles, *Like A Child* p.59.

THE WAYS AND WORDS

16. Matt Redman, 'If You Know You Are Loved By The King' from the album, *Beautiful News*, 2007.

THROUGH THE YEAR 1

17. Adrian Warnock, *Raised with Christ* (Wheaton Illinois: Crossway Books, Good News Publishers, 2010) p.13.

THROUGH THE YEAR 2

18. C.S. Lewis, *The Weight of Glory* Copyright © C.S. Lewis Pte Ltd. 1949. Used with permission.
19. Maggie Durran, *Dear God, Most Of The Time Your Quite Nice,* (London: Fount Paperbacks, 1985) p.27.
20. *Iona Abbey Worship Book* (Glasgow: Wild Goose Publications, 2001).
21. Geoffrey A. Studdert Kennedy, ed. Kerry Walters, *After War, Is Faith Possible? The Life and Message of Geoffrey 'Woodbine Willie' Studdert Kennedy* (Cascade, 2008).
22. Stephen H Travis. *I Believe In The Second Coming Of Jesus* (London: Hodder and Stoughton, 1982) p.123.
23. ChurchAds.Net 'Christmas Starts With Christ' campaign. www.churchads.net

BIBLIOGRAPHY

Reference and other books also used for background reading,
or consulted to verify quotes and prayers:

Ashwin, Angela. *The Book of a Thousand Prayers*
(Michigan: Zondervan, 2002)
Batchelor, Mary. *The Lion Prayer Collection*
(Oxford: Lion Hudson, 2001)
Benedictine monks of St Augustine's Abbey, Ramsgate.
The Book of Saints (London: Cassell, 1994)
Braybrooke, Marcus. *1000 World Prayers*
(Alresford: John Hunt Publishing Ltd, 2003)
Crystal, David (Editor). *The Cambridge Biographical Encyclopedia*
(Cambridge: Cambridge University Press, 1998)
Dobson, Derek. *Aspirations*
(Bromley: Runnymede Publishing, 1998)
Draper, Brian. *Spiritual Intelligence*
(Oxford: Lion Hudson, 2009)
Durran, Maggie. *Dear God, Most Of The Time Your Quite Nice* (London:
Fount Paperbacks, 1985)
Hymns and Psalms (Great Britain: Methodist Publishing House, 1993)
Iona Abbey Worship Book (Glasgow: Wild Goose Publications, 2001)
Kruger, Baxter C. *The Great Dance*
(Vancouver, Canada: Regent College Publishing, 2000)
Larsson, Flora. *Just a Moment Lord*
(Basingstoke: Marshall, Morgan & Scott, 1973)
Lewis, C.S. *Mere Christianity* (New York: Collier Books, 1952)
Lewis, C.S. *The Weight of Glory* (New York: Touchstone, 1996)
Logos Bible Software 4.3 SR-8
London, H.B. (Jr.) *Refresh Renew Revive*
(Colorado Springs: Focus On The Family Publishing 1996)
McKenzie, E.C. *14,000 Quips and Quotes*
(Eastbourne: Monarch Publications, 1991)
Miles, Tony and Frances. *Like A Child*
(Loughton, Essex: Rooftops Publishing, 2003)
Miles, Tony. *Maybe Today* (Farnham, Surrey: CWR, 2009)

Muller, Wayne. *Sabbath Rest* (Oxford: Lion Publishing, 2000)

Northumbria Community, *Celtic Daily Prayer*
(London: HarperCollins Publishers, 2005)

Partington, Angela (Editor). *The Oxford Dictionary of Quotations*
(Oxford, New York: Oxford University Press, 1996)

Paterson, Robert. *The Monarch Book of Christian Wisdom* (Crowborough:
Monarch Publications, 1997)

Pepper, Margaret. *The Pan Dictionary of Religious Quotations* (London:
Pan Books, 1991)

Rohr, Richard. *Falling Upward*
(San Francisco: Jossey-Bass, Wiley, 2011)

Schwartz, Tony. *The Way We're Working Isn't Working* (London: Simon &
Schuster, 2010)

Shattock, Geoff. *Jesus And The Racing Rat*
(Jacksonville, Florida: Worktalk, 2009)

Singing The Faith (London: On behalf of Trustees for Methodist Church
Purposes by Hymns Ancient & Modern)

SPCK Book of Christian Prayer
(London: Society for Promoting Christian Knowledge, 1995)

The Methodist Worship Book
(Peterborough: Methodist Publishing House, 1999)

Travis, Stephen H. *I Believe In The Second Coming Of Jesus* (London:
Hodder and Stoughton, 1982)

Tutu, Desmond. *An African Prayer Book*
(New York: Doubleday, 1995)

Warnock, Adrian. *Raised with Christ*
(Wheaton, Illinois: Crossway Books, 2010)

Zundel, Veronica. *The Lion Book Of Famous Prayers*
(Tring: Lion Publishing, 1983)

Other books, commentaries, and dictionaries were consulted when the
material was originally written for broadcast or for use in worship, but
not all sources were recorded at the time. This is a collection and some of
the content was not originally written for publication.

PEOPLE INDEX

TM = Tony Miles (Anthony D. Miles)
Hannah Sarah Miles = Tony's daughter

PEOPLE INDEX

BIBLICAL INDEX

Biblical Reference: Thought No.

THE AUTHOR –
A SHORT BIOGRAPHY

Tony Miles is married to Frances
and they have two young adult
children, Hannah and Jonathan.
He is the deputy Superintendent
Minister of Methodist Central Hall,
Westminster. He is also a Media
Chaplain and broadcaster. Tony
has been a presenter with Premier
Radio since October 1997 and is
a contributor to BBC Radio 2's
Pause For Thought.

Maybe Tomorrow is Tony's second book for CWR and follows
Maybe Today (published in 2009). Tony is also a contributor
to *Living Light* (published by the Nationwide Christian Trust).
Prior to this, with his wife, Frances, he wrote *Like A Child*
which was published by Rooftops Publishing in 2003. Tony is
a founding trustee and Vice-Chair of the Church and Media
Network, a trustee of Methodist Central Hall, Westminster,
and the Chigwell Riding Trust for Special Needs. He is
actively involved with many other organisations – including
ChurchAds.Net and the Essex Churches' Media Group. Tony is
committed to family life which includes encouraging Jonathan
in his football and Hannah in her acting and writing. He is a
member of the Rotary Club of Loughton and Buckhurst Hill,
and his interests include popular music, holidays, Fulham
Football Club, writing and swimming.

Tony's website is **www.tonymiles.com**
Twitter: **@revtonymiles**

Courses and seminars

Publishing and new media

Conference facilities

Transforming lives

CWR's vision is to enable people to experience personal transformation through applying God's Word to their lives and relationships.

Our Bible-based training and resources help people around the world to:
- Grow in their walk with God
- Understand and apply Scripture to their lives
- Resource themselves and their church
- Develop pastoral care and counselling skills
- Train for leadership
- Strengthen relationships, marriage and family life and much more.

Our insightful writers provide daily Bible-reading notes and other resources for all ages, and our experienced course designers and presenters have gained an international reputation for excellence and effectiveness.

CWR's Training and Conference Centre in Surrey, England, provides excellent facilities in an idyllic setting – ideal for both learning and spiritual refreshment.

CWR Applying God's Word
to everyday life and relationships

CWR, Waverley Abbey House,
Waverley Lane, Farnham,
Surrey GU9 8EP, UK

Telephone: +44 (0)1252 784700
Email: info@cwr.org.uk
Website: www.cwr.org.uk

Registered Charity No 294387
Company Registration No 1990308